PROSPERITY?
Seeking the True Gospel

Michael Otieno Maura
Conrad Mbewe
Ken Mbugua
John Piper
Wayne Grudem

Africa Christian Textbooks Registered Trustees
The Gospel Coalition
2015

Prosperity? Seeking the True Gospel

Published by Africa Christian Textbooks Registered Trustees. Copyright ©2015 All rights reserved.

ISBN: 978-9966-1655-3-4

The mission of Africa Christian TextbookS (ACTS) is to strengthen the church in Africa by providing evangelical, relevant and affordable literature for Christian leaders and Bible students in order to advance the cause of Christ. www.actskenya.org | acts.bookshop@gmail.com

ACTS main bookshop in Kenya is located at Africa International University (AIU), Karen, Nairobi.

Contact ACTS in Nigeria at ACTS Bookshop, International HQ, TCNN, PMB 2020, Bukuru 930008, Plateau State, Nigeria.
www.acts-ng.com | acts.jos@gmail.com

Published in partnership with The Gospel Coalition.
www.thegospelcoalition.org

Book Design by Beau Walsh, The Cultural North | www.culturalnorth.us

Contents

PREFACE

This book has been published as a result of a partnership between The Gospel Coalition and Africa Christian Textbooks Registered Trustees (Kenya).

The book builds on the foundation of the earlier title *Gaining the World, Losing the Soul* which was first published in 2012. Over the last few years new chapters have been added and the original chapters have been updated and revised.

This book has been written to counter the great damage that the so called "prosperity" or "health and wealth" gospel is doing in Africa and around the world. Some preachers are making promises of worldly prosperity to men and women and leading them far away from the Lord Jesus Christ and the genuine gospel that is found in the Bible. So widespread is this false teaching that many people may not even realise that they have been influenced by it.

Our task in this book is to address the core principles and ideas of this prosperity teaching, rather than argue with particular preachers. But there are many influential people we have in mind who, in different ways and forms, have articulated and spread this prosperity gospel (we reference some examples in Appendix III). More than anything else, we encourage readers to examine the preaching they hear in the light of the Bible. This book strives to help you do that.

Through this book, our desire is that those who have been deceived or confused by prosperity preaching will come instead to cherish the gospel of the Bible and find salvation in Jesus Christ. We also hope that this book will equip Christians to speak out against the false teaching they hear proclaimed from many pulpits. We pray that prosperity teachers themselves would read this book. We believe that some of them need to repent of their errors and submit to and embrace Jesus Christ as their saviour, while others need to learn how to properly handle the Bible as the word of God.

This is a deadly serious issue and we publish this book with a sense of urgency. We know that Peter used strong language in his second letter to condemn arrogant and greedy teachers who took advantage of Christians. As we see teachers around us today leading people astray with unbiblical and ungodly promises, we cannot stand by and do nothing. With this book we point you to our sovereign God and his perfect gospel. On this we stand against the prosperity gospel.

We are grateful to Michael Otieno Maura, Ken Mbugua and Conrad Mbewe for giving their time and energy to writing these chapters as well as to their churches for allowing them to devote that time and energy to this task.

We are thankful to Baker Publishing Group for allowing the publication of the chapters by John Piper and Wayne Grudem.

We are also very grateful to Caleb Nakina for his review of the whole book and for his editing.

Once again we have been saved by our friend David Reynolds who pulled everything together at the end and completed the final edit. This book was made possible because of the hard work that David put into *Gaining the World, Losing the Soul* back in 2012. Thanks David!

It has been a privilege to partner with The Gospel Coalition in this project. It has been a delight to work with Bill Walsh and also with his son Beau who designed the cover of the book and formatted the chapters. We are so grateful for Bill's leadership and patience.

This book would not have been published without generous donations from many people. We are thankful and praise God.

Africa Christian Textbooks Registered Trustees
The Gospel Coalition

A False Gospel

Kenneth Mbugua

I am astonished that you are so quickly deserting him who called you in the grace of Christ and are turning to a different gospel—not that there is another one, but there are some who trouble you and want to distort the gospel of Christ. But even if we or an angel from heaven should preach to you a gospel contrary to the one we preached to you, let him be accursed. As we have said before, so now I say again: If anyone is preaching to you a gospel contrary to the one you received, let him be accursed. For am I now seeking the approval of man, or of God? Or am I trying to please man? If I were still trying to please man, I would not be a servant of Christ. For I would have you know, brothers, that the gospel that was preached by me is not man's gospel. For I did not receive it from any man, nor was I taught it, but I received it through a revelation of Jesus Christ. (Galatians 1:6-12)

If even an angel preaches a gospel contrary to God's word, he is under a curse. There is not a Christian in the world that does not need to seriously consider Paul's words to the Galatians. The gospel is the church's most precious gift to cherish, protect, and pass on. And so as Christians, and particularly preachers, we must never stop checking what we believe and preach and then asking the question: *is this the gospel?* Is this the gospel that God has revealed to us in the Bible? That is what we seek to do in this book.

This book is not based on our ideas. It is not personal; we are not pitting ourselves against other preachers in a contest of egos. Like Paul, we seek to not preach ourselves, but Christ (2 Cor. 4:5). We labour to base all that we write on the authority of the word of God revealed in the Bible. We strain to not twist it for our own purposes, but to handle it faithfully (2 Cor. 4:2).

And as we carefully read the gospel that we have received in the Bible, we have come to the conclusion that there is a false gospel—the prosperity gospel—sweeping our continent. Across Africa, there are many churches preaching this false gospel. It is a dangerous lie wrapped in a covering of religion. Those affected by it are being led away from God's good news to a man-centred deception. Paul took nothing more seriously than the danger of a different gospel and we feel the same way. Nothing is more serious; our souls depend on it.

We write this book to address those who preach this false gospel, and those who have bought into it, praying that God would grant us patience, kindness, wisdom, and gentleness as we humbly seek to correct error, bringing us all under the authority of God's word.

We will not sugarcoat the truth. Paul was most fierce and sharp when dealing with those who were corrupting the gospel. As he did, we want to urge believers to reject a "different gospel" that is not the gospel. This message will be hard for many to hear. And one of the reasons it will be hard is that the voices of influential and trusted men lend their support to this false gospel.

But it is not big names that count. Large congregations, celebrity status, and wide influence have never been the mark of what is true. We must stand on the revelation of Scripture and not shape our gospel according to the approval of the crowd. Paul warned the Galatians not to believe *anyone* who preaches a gospel different to the one given him by Christ—not even an angel. That is our concern too. We entreat you in love; humbly receive the word of God. It can save your soul (James 1:21).

What is the prosperity gospel? It is a 'gospel' claiming freedom from sickness, poverty, and all suffering on the basis of Christ's death on the cross. Promising material, physical, and visible blessings for all who would embrace it, the prosperity gospel insists that God's will is for all his children to prosper here and now. But this prosperity gospel contains four crucial distortions that are four differences from the biblical gospel. It proclaims a small God; it fails to identify man's greatest need; it empties the gospel of its power; and it robs God of his glory.

Distortion One: A Small God

What do you long for the most? The answer to this question will help you identify your god. Preachers of the prosperity gospel call people to turn to Jesus. But the motivation they give people is health, wealth, husbands, wives, jobs, and promotions. In this false gospel, we are not persuaded to desire, pursue, or treasure Jesus. Instead, Jesus is regarded as merely the way to get the material things our worldly hearts hunger for. And what your heart desires more than God has become your god.

Scripture is clear that the goal of our salvation is God, not gold. Knowing him, being united to him, and being reconciled with him are the purposes to which the Bible points us. "For Christ also suffered once for sins, the righteous for the unrighteous, that he might bring us to God" (1 Pet. 3:18). Take note of the word *that* in this verse; it helps us understand why Christ suffered and died. He suffered and died *in order that he might bring us to God.*

Jesus Christ himself perfectly summed up the heart and purpose of our salvation in his prayer to the Father: "this is eternal life, that they know you the only true God, and Jesus Christ whom you have sent" (John 17:3). When Paul taught the Colossians about the glory of God's work in us, he centred on our union with Christ. "To them God chose to make known how great among the Gentiles are the riches of the glory of this mystery, which is Christ in you, the hope of glory" (Col. 1:27).

The gospel is about an infinitely great God who offers us the best gift imaginable: himself. That is the incredible beauty of the gospel—sinners can know God and enjoy him forever. God's people through the ages have understood that there is nothing better. But the prosperity gospel reduces God to a sugar daddy by treating material gifts as the purpose of the gospel. The temporary benefits of material prosperity are not what Jesus died to win for us.

Jesus died to bring us back to God. And the heart of the salvation he bought for us is that we can know God in a deep and personal way. Can you see why a message that exchanges *God* in these statements with *wealth, health,* and *prosperity* is offering us a little God who is no God at all? Wealth, health, and prosperity are not the glory of the gospel, they are not the purpose for which Christ died, and they are inferior gifts compared to fellowship with Almighty God. These are the very things the world pursues; they are false gods. To preach that temporary and material blessings are the purpose of our salvation turns Christianity into idolatry and trades in the glory of God for a cheap substitute.

Distortion Two: Our Greatest Need

When you visit a hospital because of illness, the doctor's most important task is to diagnose the cause of your symptoms. If he gets the source of your problem wrong, then his solution will also be wrong. Moreover, such a 'solution' could lead to even greater suffering. In order to truly bless people, we also need to correctly diagnose their greatest need.

What is humanity's greatest need? What problem did God address when he sent his only son to die? The prosperity preacher points people to their physical, financial, and relational struggles as the main problem that requires fixing. Christ is then preached only as a means for solving those problems, even though the Bible is clear about man's greatest problem. It is far worse than being broke or hungry.

One of the most famous miracles happened when Jesus fed five thousand people with five loaves and two fish. But many people do not know what happened after the crowd had been fed. Amazed by what they saw, the crowd decided that they needed to lead a coup and make Jesus their king (John 6:15). Did they have the right idea of the gospel? Not according to Jesus. The crowd zealously sought Jesus to the point of jumping into boats to follow him across the lake (John 6:22-24). But, when at last they found him, he did not commend them. Jesus saw their motives and strongly rebuked them:

> *Truly, truly, I say to you, you are seeking me, not because you saw signs, but because you ate your fill of the loaves. Do not work for the food that per-ishes, but for the food that endures to eternal life, which the Son of Man will give to you. For on him God the Father has set his seal. (John 6:26-27)*

They were following Jesus for material advantage. Jesus performed signs and wonders in order that people would believe in him and receive eternal life (John 20:30-31). But these people were more interested in a free lunch. They thought the Messiah would give them all they want-ed in this life, but they were missing the incomparably better thing that he offered. If you are following Jesus for material benefits, you have failed to identify your greatest need.

So Jesus is clear; health and wealth are not our great-est needs. But what is? In order to understand this, we have to go back to basics: who is God and who are we? In Romans 1, we are reminded that God is righteous and we are sinful. And because of God's righteousness and our wickedness, his just judgement stands against us. If I understand that the almighty and holy God is angry with me, then my financial struggles, relationship stresses, and career ambitions can no longer be my first priority. My sin problem becomes the priority.

What exactly is this sin problem? Again, Romans 1 is helpful. It explains that although we know God, in our corrupt nature we do not glorify him as we should. Instead, we give the glory that belongs to the Creator to what he has created (Rom. 1:22-23). This idolatry is the heart of sin. Our greatest need is to fix the problem of sin.

When we grasp that all the pains of life are symptoms of our real disease, our God-defying sin, we will seek a gospel that addresses not just the symptoms but the root cause. We need God to forgive our sins, take his wrath away from us, and make us right in his sight. This is what we need both now and for eternity. When the preacher, as a spiritual doctor, misdiagnoses the problem, he treats his patients with a false gospel that, like bad medicine, just makes them worse.

Distortion Three: Emptying the Gospel of its Power

When Paul wrote to the church in Corinth, he was correcting problems that we see all around us today. The Corinthians had received the pure gospel from the lips of the Apostle Paul (1 Cor. 15:1-4), but over time their preachers had changed the message in order to suit the audience. And as they modified the gospel message, they did not just change its emphasis; they emptied the gospel of its power.

Churches that preach the prosperity gospel make a similar mistake. Their preachers might mention the cross in their preaching and even say that Christ died for our sins. But they say that the purpose of Christ's death was our healing and prosperity. Of course, this is a relevant issue to any congregation. Many people are suffering and struggling with financial or health issues. We all have material needs and desires. It is an appealing message: *come to Jesus and have your best life now*. But it is an inferior message because it lacks the power that the real gospel has to save men, women, and children *from their sins* (Matt. 1:21).

People do not like to be told they are wretched sinners destined for hell. We prefer to hear about how we can get promoted at work, get ahead in the world, and get quick fixes for our earthly troubles. Therefore, a gospel that does not emphasize these things does not make any sense to many people (1 Cor. 1:18). And that is because, naturally, we are spiritually blind and have no sense of the eternal beauty of God. But instead of wielding the gospel that God uses to awaken sinners to the glory, beauty, and salvation of God, prosperity preachers abandon the gospel and seek only to satisfy godless desires. Their message does not and cannot save. Prosperity preaching swaps the power of the gospel for a powerless message.

If you believe that Christ saves you in order to give you prosperity in this life, then you have put your hope in a powerless message. Unlike God's good news revealed to us in the Bible, the prosperity gospel can neither save your soul (Rom. 1:16) nor give you life (2 Tim. 1:9-10). It cannot grant you peace with God (Rom. 5:1), or reconcile you to him (2 Cor. 5:18-20). The prosperity gospel cannot bring you into God's family (John 1:12-13), give you hope for eternity (Col. 1:21-23), or secure your resurrection to life (John 11:25-27). But the power of the gospel is that God can save you *forever* by changing your status from a hell-bound subject of wrath to an eternally justified child of God. That is power.

If you have turned away from preaching the cross, you have turned away from the only message that has the power to save anyone from sin. Christ had to die because it was the only way to pay the price for our sin. Does that new house, car, or job require the death of the Son of God? The prosperity gospel might seem relevant and it certainly is popular, but by focusing on material blessings it misses the point of the gospel and robs the gospel message of its essential purpose and power.

Distortion Four: Robbing God of his Glory

The most basic mistake every person has made is to think: *I am the centre of the universe.* When we read the Bible, we realise not only that God made everything, but also that the creation is about *him.* The Bible and the gospel itself relentlessly point us to God. And when we think about the reality of God in the world and in the Bible, the word we most often use is *glory.* We cannot understand either the seriousness of sin or the design and purpose of the gospel until we grasp the glory of God.

God's glory is his overflowing and overwhelming nature and character. His glory includes his infinite attributes of holiness, righteousness, love, justice, grace, mercy, purity, beauty, power, and wisdom. And the happy duty that comes with being alive in this world that God created by and for his glory *is to glorify him.* The purpose of our lives is to focus on, draw attention to, live for, and delight in God's glory. God deserves this from us. When we rob God of his glory, it does not mean that God be-

comes less glorious; that is impossible. But it means that
we fail to glorify him as we should.

As we looked at man's greatest need, we saw that refusing to glorify God, while glorifying what he has created, is at the heart of sin that separates us from our maker.
When the prosperity gospel obscures this understanding
of sin, it fails to point us to the glory of God as the missing
focus of our lives.

When prosperity preachers emphasise material needs,
they do not lead people to repentance because their message does not put people in awe of that glory. Instead
of teaching us what God deserves from us, prosperity
preaching encourages us to think of what we will get from
God. Jumping for joy about how God will make you rich
and strong is not worshiping God. A wrong definition of
man's greatest problem robs God of His glory.

Therefore, the prosperity gospel also robs God of
his glory by misunderstanding the *design* of the gospel.
Paul explained the purpose and design of the gospel in
Ephesians 1:3-14. In Christ, we have been chosen by God
before the foundation of the world (1:4), predestined to be
adopted as sons (1:5), redeemed through his blood, for-
given (1:7), enlightened (1:9), sealed with the Holy Spirit
(1:13), and guaranteed a heavenly inheritance (1:14). No
wonder it is called good news. And from beginning to end
this gospel of God is "to the praise of his glory" (1:6, 12,
14).

The gospel reconciles us to God. It takes away the
hurdles that keep us from God, enabling us to be in an intimate relationship with God in which we can glorify him
forever. And the Father has made these blessings avail-
able to us in his Son (look for the phrase "in Christ" or its
equivalent in Ephesians 1). None of these blessings can be

enjoyed outside of Christ because it is his perfect life and work on the cross that bought these blessings for us. At every point, the design of the gospel directs us away from glorying in ourselves (Eph. 2:8-9) and points us toward the glory of God as our hope and purpose.

The gospel glorifies God. The blessings of the gospel that we mentioned (chosen, adopted, redeemed, for-given, etc.) all bring us to God. And these blessings are only through the Son of God, purchased by him in a way that magnifies God's gracious mercy and love. They cannot be earned; they can only be received, so we realize where the glory belongs. As we look exclusively to Christ for the eternal blessings that we could never provide for ourselves, we are left with no one to glorify except God (1 Cor. 1:30-31).

But the prosperity gospel robs God of His glory at every step. It does so by redefining the blessings received in Christ. Those who hear its message go home desiring earthly treasures instead of fellowship with God. When earthly treasure is desired more than God, the treasure receives the glory that only God deserves. In the parable of the hidden treasure in Matthew 13:44, the man sells all his earthly possessions to get the kingdom of heaven. The prosperity gospel offers us the opposite deal.

The prosperity gospel goes further in robbing God of his glory by turning its audience away from *Christ's sufficiency*. Instead of Christ alone, prosperity preachers advertise many methods of obtaining blessing like anointing oil, "planting a seed", 'holy water', and prayers from 'the man of God'. This false gospel downplays Christ's sufficiency by claiming that rituals and men are channels of blessings from God outside of Christ Jesus. Such a message denies that he is at the centre and robs God of his glory.

When we seek blessings outside of Christ that do not glorify God, we also dislodge the cross from the heart of the Bible. The Scripture teaches us that God's master plan of bringing glory to his name has the cross as its centre. The Old Testament is full of signs and types that point us to Christ and his work on the cross (Luke 24:27). The sacrificial system teaches us our greatest need and prepares us for Christ (Heb. 9). The prophets prophesied of his coming and his sufferings (1 Pet. 1:10-12). And for eternity we will never stop remembering and glorifying Jesus' sacrifice (Rev. 5:6 & 12).

The cross is at the centre of God's plan to show and share his glory forever. But prosperity preachers go through the Bible highlighting all the earthly blessings that God's people enjoyed. And, in direct conflict with Christ's handling of Scripture (e.g. Luke 24:27), they make these earthly blessings the main point of the Bible. This turns people away from the centrality of the cross of Christ and robs God of His glory. There is no more serious charge against a message then: *it takes glory from God.*

Conclusion

The prosperity gospel is a dangerous message because, while pretending to bring good news, it offers a false gospel that leads people away from God. It presents a small God who is valued as the means to material benefits. It misdiagnoses our greatest problem—sin and separation from God—and fails to identify and address our greatest need. This so-called gospel is powerless to save us as it diverts our attention from the glory of God to human inventions and temporary blessings. The prosperity gospel glorifies man and the things of this world instead of God. That makes it a false gospel.

CHAPTER 1

Misunderstanding the Bible

Kenneth Mbugua

There are some things in them that are hard to understand, which the ignorant and unstable twist to their own destruction, as they do the other Scriptures. You therefore, beloved, knowing this beforehand, take care that you are not carried away with the error of lawless people and lose your own stability. (2 Peter 3:16-17)

The falsehood of the prosperity gospel is rooted in misinterpretation of the Bible. The word of God has been twisted, both unintentionally and intentionally, and the result is a deceptive man-made message. If you are genuinely pursuing the truth and humbly approaching his word, God can set you free from the lies of this empty, false gospel and give you life in him. My confidence rests on Christ's promise in John 8:31-32: "If you abide in my word, you are truly my disciples, and you will know the truth, and the truth will set you free."

God has revealed truth to us in the Bible. But this truth has plenty of competition; our deceitful hearts (Jer. 17:9), the Devil who is "the deceiver of the whole world" (Rev. 12:9), and a world full of lies. As Christians, we constantly have to remember that truth is not determined by a vote, a point of view, or a popularity contest. God has revealed truth to us and we must labour to understand what he is telling us. How can we do this?

We must come to the Bible asking, 'what does God intend to communicate through this passage?' That is the question we ask when we read each other's letters and text messages. We read the whole message, try to determine what the author meant, keep in mind other things that person has written to us, and seek clarity on unfamiliar words. When we are clear on the meaning of the message, we respond appropriately.

But many preachers treat the words of God with less care than they would a friend's text message. Prosperity gospel preachers regularly approach God's word as though it can mean whatever they decide it means. Sentences are taken out of context, the rest of the Bible is ignored, and words are twisted. If people read our letters and text messages in the same way, we would also be misunderstood. We cannot afford to make this mistake with the most important message. Do not miss out on God's gospel because you are too busy trying to come up with your own version of the good news.

If you attend a church where you hear the prosperity gospel, you will find it hard to believe that it is not the gospel. After all, you will have memorized verses in the Bible that seem to confirm this prosperity theology. But the problem is not in the verses you learn but in the way prosperity preachers are misinterpreting them.

In this chapter, we want to address some of the most common misinterpretations of the Bible which preachers use to proclaim the prosperity gospel. We want to look for what God is really saying to us in these texts by studying their contexts and drawing meaning out from them, rather than imposing our own interpretations on them. We need to treat God's words with reverence and care.

His Poverty and Our Riches

Let us begin with 2 Corinthians 8:9: "For you know the grace of our Lord Jesus Christ, that though he was rich, yet for your sake he became poor, so that you by his poverty might become rich." Prosperity preachers use this verse to proclaim that Christ died so that we could be wealthy. But if you read the context of 2 Corinthians 8, you soon discover that it is about Christians giving to others. Furthermore, the Christians that Paul was asking the Corinthians to emulate in their sacrificial giving were themselves very poor.

We want you to know, brothers, about the grace of God that has been given among the churches of Macedonia, for in a severe test of affliction, their abundance of joy and their extreme poverty have overflowed in a wealth of generosity on their part. (2 Cor. 8:1-2)

Paul is holding up, as an example of godliness, the poor Christians in Macedonia who still sacrificed to meet the needs of others. Then in the ninth verse of the chapter,

to make his point, Paul compared them to the far greater
example of the one who sacrificed himself for our good.

It is completely wrong, therefore, to read this chapter
and conclude that it is about *us getting rich*. On the contrary, giving us two examples to follow, God is teaching us
through the Apostle Paul that we should live sacrificially
and generously. The joy of both the Macedonians and
Christ did not come from wealth, but from the love of God
that enabled them to give extravagantly *for others' needs*.

But what then are the riches that this verse says Christ
gave up and Christians will have? Did Christ give up material wealth to become our Saviour? The Bible, and basic
logic, clearly show us that this is *not* what Christ gave up.

> *Let each of you look not only to his own inter-*
> *ests, but also to the interests of others. Have this*
> *mind among yourselves, which is yours in Christ*
> *Jesus, who, though he was in the form of God,*
> *did not count equality with God a thing to be*
> *grasped, but emptied himself, by taking the form*
> *of a servant, being born in the likeness of men.*
> *(Phil. 2:4-7)*

Christ was indeed poor while he was on this earth,
as the Gospels frequently show (Luke 9:58). But, as the
above text explains, Christ lowered himself by leaving
heaven and *the intimate spiritual communion and glory*
with his Father that he enjoyed there in order to come
to this world as a man. This is far greater than material
wealth. The riches that Christ (temporarily) gave up for us
were heavenly and spiritual riches. And, ultimately, these
are the riches that Christ died to win for us: reconciliation
and communion with God (John 17:24).

But in the age to come, according to Revelation 21, there will be streets of gold in the New Jerusalem (21:21). Is that then a Christian's motivation for wanting to be in that city? Keep reading and two verses later you will see that the glory of the Father and the Lamb will light up heaven (21:23). Surely, *that* will be much more exciting for the Christian.

If you doubt the Bible's emphasis, look for references to material blessing in the book of Revelation and then look for references to the glory and worship of God. The heart that loves God longs for the day when we will be caught up in worship and adoration of him. And saints who are satisfied in God will want to sacrificially give as the Macedonians and Jesus Christ did, instead of worrying about what they can accumulate now.

Health and Healing

A verse that is often used to suggest that God will make us healthy is Isaiah 53:5: "But he was pierced for our transgressions; he was crushed for our iniquities; upon him was the chastisement that brought us peace, and with his wounds we are healed." Note, firstly, that this verse and the verses around it describe the suffering of the messiah and his sacrificial death for us. Why did Christ suffer and die? The verse clearly explains that he died for our transgressions and iniquities—our sins. If he died for our sins, then what is the nature of the healing that his death brings? The clear meaning of the text is that we have been healed of our sinful guilt by Christ's sacrifice.

As the Apostle Peter said, "He himself bore our sins in his body on the tree, that we might die to sin and live to righteousness. By his wounds you have been healed" (1

Pet. 2:24). Dying to sin and living in righteousness; that is the eternal and amazing healing that Christ's sacrifice won for us.

It is also true that, as the Bible explains, Christ's work on the cross has implications for all suffering. By dealing with our sin, he made sure that the consequences of our sin which has corrupted the world, including suffering, would also be removed. But God is equally clear in his word that this glorious completion of the work of redemption will not occur until he comes again and brings this present age to an end (Rom. 8:18-25 & 1 Cor. 15:20-28). The benefits of Christ's work are not all enjoyed on this earth.

One day our bodies will be glorified and the earth shall be restored and there will be no more tears. Faith in that sure future gives us strength to endure the pains of this world: "the sufferings of this present time are not worth comparing with the glory that is to be revealed to us" (Rom. 8:18). There will be no escape from suffering for as long as we live in our corrupted bodies in a broken world, but we confidently look forward to the time when everything will be right.

But are there signs of hope now that remind us that suffering, due to Christ's work, will be completely removed? Yes, absolutely. There is a reason why the gospel writer described physical healing as a fulfillment of Isaiah 53:4 (Matt. 8:17). And there is a reason why Jesus went about healing bodies as well as forgiving sins. John MacArthur helps make the connection between healing, the suffering of Christ, and our suffering:

Isaiah was saying that the Messiah would bear the consequences of the sins of men, namely the

griefs and sorrows of life ... Matthew found an
analogical fulfillment of these words in Jesus'
healing ministry because sickness results from sin
for which the Servant paid with His life (vv. 7,8;
cf. 1 Pet. 2:24). In eternity, all sickness will be re-
moved, so ultimately it is included in the benefits of
the atonement.[i]

Christ's healing ministry fulfilled prophecy, demonstrated his power, and proved he is God. But healing bodies was not the purpose; it was a means to the end. The end
was that we would believe in Christ for the forgiveness of
our sins and be reconciled to God (John 20:30-31). Our
God does still heal from illness. God still performs miracles. And we can be certain that one day there will be no
disease and no suffering. But let us not misuse the Bible
to claim promises that God has not given.

God has not promised a life now without suffering. But
he has promised us grace in (2 Cor. 12:9-10) and ultimate
good through (Rom. 8:28) our suffering. Like the Apostle
Paul we hold on in suffering to the hope of resurrection
(Phil. 3:10-11). We put our faith in the gospel and cling on
to the confidence that we have in Christ that will outlast
any pain we have in this life.[ii]

Our Prayers and God's Promises

As Christians face the hardships of life, they pray to
God for strength, guidance, and help. Prayer is an essen-

---

i   *The MacArthur Study Bible*, ed. John MacArthur, Jr., electronic
ed. (Nashville: Word, 1997), Is. 53:4.

ii We will look at this in more detail in the chapter on suffering.

tial part of the life of every believer and every church. But the health of a prayer life is not determined by a word count. *What* we pray for reveals our hearts. Churches that preach the prosperity gospel often include long prayer services—and that is a good thing. But the substance of our prayers is more important than their length.

Prosperity preachers encourage churches to base prayers on misunderstood promises and to pray them for the wrong motives. The promise that Christians can ask anything of the Father and he will give it to them is found in several places in the Gospels. It is one of the most incredible promises in the Bible, and it is much better than preachers of the prosperity gospel realise.

God promises to answer the prayers of his children. That is what the verses say and that is what they mean. But that is also not *all* that the verses say and mean. Let us take a closer look at John 15:7: "If you abide in me, and my words abide in you, ask whatever you wish, and it will be done for you."

The verse begins with a condition: *if you abide in me and my words abide in you.* If you remove this condition from the sentence, you will inevitably misunderstand the promise. If we live in Jesus Christ and his words live in us, then the things that we ask for will be God's pleasure to provide. God's word is God's will that has been revealed to us. And as we immerse ourselves in Jesus, as God's word has revealed him, to the point where his desires are our desires, then our own will shall be conformed to his will. When this has occurred, we will truly desire and pray for what God wants.

This is the same logic that we see in another misunderstood verse: "And we know that for those who love God all things work together for good" (Rom. 8:28). Does

this mean that God gives me anything that I want? Look
again. The people referred to in this verse are *those who
love him*. If you love God, you want God's glory and his
will in your life more than anything. And this is a desire
that God is eager and willing to fulfill. Jesus Christ himself demonstrated this when he prayed: "My Father, if it
be possible, let this cup pass from me; nevertheless, not as
I will, but as you will" (Matt. 26:39). In his humanity, he
wanted release from suffering. But there was something
he wanted even more than that—his Father's will and glory. This is the kind of prayer that God delights to receive.

The Bible clearly teaches that God does what he pleases: "Whatever the LORD pleases, he does, in heaven and
on earth, in the seas and all deeps" (Ps. 135:6). But in
Christ Jesus, his pleasure and ours come together. When
we immerse our lives in his word, God transforms us by
his Spirit and shapes our desires, values, and passions to
be like his. These things define our will, which we make
known to God in prayer.

Does this make the promise of John 15 less remark-
able? On the contrary, the sovereign God has chosen to
carry out his will through Christians' prayers: "for it is
God who works in you, both to will and to work for his
good pleasure" (Phil. 2:13). He has chosen to make your
prayers powerful. God does *not* say: 'don't bother praying
because I will do what is best without you.' Instead, he
delights in doing what is best *through our prayers*. He
changes hearts so that people want his perfect will and
when Christians pray their godly desires to him, he loves
to take action.

The Bible is full of good examples of God's people
praying God's will. Look at how Daniel's prayers, for in-
stance, were informed by God's word. In Daniel 9, we read

that he discovered God's prophecy that the desolation of Jerusalem would end after seventy years; a time that was fast approaching. Did that make Daniel complacent? No, it inspired him to pray. Daniel's response was to fast and pray to God that he would do his will. God was pleased to hear Daniel and answer his prayers as the exiles returned home. This is how God works and this is how we should pray.

We need to take care to interpret John 15 and similar texts in the light of what the Bible teaches us about how God works out his sovereign will through our prayers. When our hearts are immersed in God's word, we will desire God's will and glory above our own so that we will pray like Christ in the garden of Gethsemane. But if we lose sight of God's will and become obsessed with our own godless desires, then we are not living in Jesus Christ. And we cannot claim God's help while opposing his will. God has a great design for prayer; we do not want to miss out on it in selfish misinterpretation of his word.

Sowing and Reaping

One of the most misused concepts in the Bible has been *sowing and reaping*. In many churches it is marketed as the "reaping and sowing principle". Two of the verses most commonly used to support it are 2 Corinthians 9:6 ("Whoever sows sparingly will also reap sparingly, and whoever sows bountifully will also reap bountifully") and Galatians 6:7 ("Do not be deceived: God is not mocked, for whatever one sows, that will he also reap"). What is the message of these verses?

We should firstly note that these verses are simple to understand. They mean what they say and they are designed to motivate our sowing by the prospect of our reaping. That is how life works. We all want to live in a way that produces benefit. There is no point sowing, if we do not hope to reap. The problem with the preachers of the prosperity gospel is not that they expect reaping to follow sowing, but that *their idea of what is to be reaped is far too small.* They think of temporary gain when they are offered permanent gain. They focus on unsatisfying benefits and miss a deeply satisfying blessing. And they preach of monetary treasures when a priceless gift is before them.

The prosperity gospel's sowing and reaping principle deviates from the Bible's teaching in many particular ways. It defies the heavenly perspective that the Bible urges us to have. This heavenly perspective ought to regulate how we sow our time, energy, talents, and money.

Do not lay up for yourselves treasures on earth, where moth and rust destroy and where thieves break in and steal, but lay up for yourselves treasures in heaven, where neither moth nor rust destroys and where thieves do not break in and steal. For where your treasure is, there your heart will be also. (Matt. 6:19-21)

The idea here is that treasure is a good thing and so we ought to aim for eternal treasure, rather than rusty, moth-eaten treasure which cannot last. What a poor gospel it is which offers us merely earthly treasure. By contrast, it has been God's people's knowledge that their treasure is in heaven that has empowered them to endure persecution and put their earthly treasure at risk. As the writer to the Hebrews testified about his believing readers, "you joyfully accepted the plundering of your property, since you knew that you yourselves had a better possession and an abiding one" (Heb. 10:34). That is the sowing and reaping which God offers his people: spiritual sowing and eternal reaping.

The prosperity gospel also promotes a love for money, while the Bible is clear about the dangers of this approach to life. The Apostle Paul's teaching on this could not be more apparent:

> *For the love of money is a root of all kinds of evils. It is through this craving that some have wandered away from the faith and pierced themselves with many pangs. But as for you, O man of God, flee these things. Pursue righteousness, godliness, faith, love, steadfastness, gentleness. (1 Tim. 6:10-11)*

A lot of what is called practicing the sowing and reaping principle is merely a cover for the love of money. But no matter how we label it, if we only focus on material things we can only expect material benefits, not spiritual ones. You do, indeed, reap what you sow. Many, in fact, have ended up reaping sorrow and pain after their practice of what they thought was a biblical principle. If we love money, as God has specifically warned us not to, we may get some fleeting pleasures and temporary benefits. But as money cannot satisfy our souls or heal our hearts, in the end this disobedient sowing will reap sadness and death.

Furthermore, the prosperity gospel's idea of sowing and reaping denies the Bible by suggesting that God has no problem with being replaced by idols. What do I mean?

When we use the Bible to justify our idolatrous pursuit of money, we make God out to be the willing supplier of our favorite idol. But God's wrath burns against people who put his beautiful glory in second place to pursue other gods. God's people seek the treasure that is God himself.

> *But whatever gain I had, I counted as loss for the sake of Christ. Indeed, I count everything as loss because of the surpassing worth of knowing Christ Jesus my Lord. For his sake I have suffered the loss of all things and count them as rubbish, in order that I may gain Christ. (Phil. 3:7-8)*

This verse would not make sense to anyone practicing the sowing and reaping principle of the prosperity gospel. Paul is saying that the very things for which the prosperity preachers encourage us to come to God are *the things he has given up in order to have God*. What do *you* prefer: riches and wealth or God? Where is your treasure?

Let us also look specifically at some of these texts that are used by prosperity preachers to justify their approach to sowing and reaping. 2 Corinthians 9:6 is located in the same passage that we looked at earlier, in which Paul was commending the Macedonians for their generous financial gift to the church in Jerusalem, despite their own poverty. What does Paul say that such generous givers should expect to receive and see in response to their generosity?

When Christians sow in generosity, they reap glory and honour to God. And there is no better harvest. Read on in 2 Corinthians 9 and you see that Paul wrote that their generosity "will produce thanksgiving to God" (9:11). In supplying the needs of God's people, they had inspired "many thanksgivings to God" (9:12). And those who have received the gift would "glorify God because of your submission" (9:13). As Jesus Christ also instructed: "let your light shine before others, so that they may see your good works and give glory to your Father who is in heaven" (Matt 5:16). The message is clear: give so that God is glorified. When we sow for God, we reap the enormous blessing of glorifying and honouring him.

But, even though it was not his focus, Paul did mention material benefits too. In what way and for what purpose did Paul describe material blessings for generous givers? Paul said that those who give will receive from God enough so that they can continue to bless others: "And God is able to make all grace abound to you, so that having all sufficiency in all things at all times, you may abound in every good work" (2 Cor. 9:8). He does not promise them luxury, but enough. And the purpose of what they receive is not to accumulate wealth, but to give: "you will be enriched in every way to be generous in every way" (9:11). If you think this text is about our monetary gain, you have entirely missed the point. God promises his children enough to serve him, not luxury to ignore him.

As for Galatians 6:7, studying its context also informs us that Paul taught something very different from the emphasis of the prosperity gospel. The text is not about getting but about giving. Christians should "bear one another's burdens" (6:2), "share all good things with the one who teaches" (6:6), "not grow weary of doing good" (6:9), and "do good to everyone" (6:10). The sowing in this chapter is clearly blessing others. So what is the reaping?

Paul mentioned the principle of sowing and reaping here as a warning of the consequences of refusing to do good. "For the one who sows to his own flesh will from the flesh reap corruption," Paul warned the Galatians, "but the one who sows to the Spirit will from the Spirit reap eternal life" (Gal. 6:8). Actually looking at the passage tells us that far from endorsing the prosperity gospel, Paul rebuked it in the strongest terms. Those who sow for God reap spiritual blessing.

If you give to others with the motive of financial gain for yourself, you are sowing to the flesh. Those who walk according to the flesh will not inherit the kingdom. But selflessly blessing others is evidence of the Spirit's work. The harvest for the godly is eternal life and the Galatians were encouraged to keep going because one day they would receive the fruit of their labour. God gives to us so that we can give to others and our reward is not material and worldly, but spiritual and eternal.

Word of Faith Theology

Another popular message of many prosperity preachers today is 'word of faith' theology. They teach that our words have the power to create reality. We can, it is said, speak health and prosperity into existence by positively confessing our desires. Once more, this false teaching is based on a fundamental misunderstanding of several Bible verses.

The faith that is exercised in this teaching is not so much faith in God as it is faith in one's own faith. You are encouraged to see yourself as the master of your own destiny. If you just believe and ask confidently, you can chart your own future and acquire the desires of your heart. When the thing claimed and believed does not materialize, the blame is laid at a lack of faith.

Although many of these preachers do not try to base their teachings on Scripture, they will sometimes quote

Hebrews 11:1 as evidence. The writer to the Hebrews says that "faith is the substance of things hoped for" (KJV). Seizing on the word "substance" (which other translations render "assurance" and "confidence"), word of faith preachers use this verse to claim that faith *creates* substance. If that were so, God would not be the only Creator; we would join him in creating by speaking our will into existence.

The answer to this misinterpretation can once again be found by treating the Bible with respect and looking at the context from which the verse is pulled. Open the book of Hebrews and it is clear that the author is *not* teaching his readers how to use the power of faith to *change* the circumstances around them. A few verses earlier, his readers are commended for having "endured a hard struggle with sufferings" (10:32) and "joyfully accepted the plundering of your property" (10:34). Then, in verse 35, the writer urges them to continue with the same confidence that they had demonstrated in those dire circumstances. What was that confidence?

It was, firstly, a faith that ran on patience not a sense of entitlement. "For you have need of endurance, so that when you have done the will of God you may receive what is promised" (10:36). The Hebrew Christians' faith was proven real when they endured, not avoided, suffering: "we are not of those who shrink back and are destroyed, but of those who have faith and preserve their souls" (10:39). Moreover, this was a confidence focused on eternal things, as is clear from the affirmation: "you knew that you yourselves had a better possession and an abiding one" (10:34). Their "great reward" was nothing as temporary as the health of a body that will die or possessions that will be left behind.

The faith of Hebrews 10 and 11 allowed these Christians to see past their present suffering to the reality of eternity prepared for them. This confidence in their future inheritance gave them the strength to *let go* of their earthly possessions. While the world lives for what it can get now, Christians have a totally different motivation.

Therefore, the examples of faith that follow in Hebrews 11 are not examples of the power of faith changing circumstances (God changes circumstances, not faith). On the contrary, they are examples of people acting on the basis of a future reality that could only be seen and possessed by faith because it was not material or earthly. It includes believers who were tortured, beaten, imprisoned, and even killed. Their faith enabled them to endure this and, after death, receive the goal and reward of their faith; the eternal glory that was awaiting them. "They desire a better country, that is, a heavenly one" (Heb. 11:16).

It is a great sin to teach believers, who are called to endure in view of an eternal reward, that they should instead seek and claim rewards now. This false teaching keeps the suffering saints away from the grace and hope that true faith contains. The word of faith message, when exposed as a lie, has also driven people away from the church and Christianity altogether. May all who have the responsibility and privilege of preaching the word of Christ remember Christ's own words: "whoever causes one of these little ones who believe in me to sin, it would be better for him to have a great millstone fastened around his neck and to be drowned in the depth of the sea" (Matt. 18:6).

Conclusion

The prosperity gospel rests on misinterpretations of the Bible that completely distort its clear meaning. In this way, it diverts Christians from serving God to worshipping themselves and trusting in a false gospel. We must treat God's word honestly and carefully so that we know the truth and can be set free by it.

When our Lord Jesus Christ left heaven and became a man, he did not give up or promise us *material* benefits. He gave up *heavenly* riches, the glory and love he shared with his Father, to come to our world so that we could share in these blessings with him forever. When Christ lived a life of suffering and then died on the cross, his punishment was designed to heal our deepest wound— our sinfulness. So God promises us something far more important and valuable than health or wealth now. Thanks to his death and resurrection, Jesus promises his people permanent reconciliation with God and a sin-free life in the age to come.

As God's people experience the salvation that is in Jesus, they want God's glory more than anything else. And God's plan is so great that he then uses the righteous desires of his people, expressed in prayer, to do his will. It should not surprise us, therefore, that the Bible encourages us also to sow generously in our deeds for spiritual motives. As we do this, he promises us an everlasting harvest prepared for us in heaven.

CHAPTER 2

True and False Prosperity

Michael Otieno Maura

When he built a city, he called the name of the city after the name of his son, Enoch. (Genesis 4:17)

> *To Seth also a son was born, and he called his name Enosh. At that time people began to call upon the name of the LORD. (Genesis 4:25-26)*

In Africa today, people are talking about prosperity. It dominates our imaginations and permeates our conversations. And as it grips our culture, it is also entering our pulpits. There are many preachers who are preaching a gospel of material prosperity. But this prosperity that grips the hearts and minds of men and women, from the streets to the churches, is a false prosperity. It is a false prosperity against which the Bible repeatedly warns us.

As far back as Genesis 4:17-26, we find a contrast between the godless family of Cain and the godly family of Seth. Cain's family could boast of great achievements and material prosperity. They appeared to be successful, but their achievements were made without reference to God. Far from God, their prosperity was temporary and fleeting; of and for this world. Seth's family did not have such material achievements to display. But they called on the name of the Lord; that was their glory. This family knew a true and lasting prosperity that was grounded in God.

In many of our pulpits today, the preaching is centred on worldly achievement and material prosperity: houses and cars, success in business, money, health, and happiness. Such preaching is in direct conflict with the word of God from Genesis through to the gospels and epistles. Our preaching should lead sinners to call upon the name of the Lord. It should lead people to cry out for mercy and salvation through the Lord Jesus Christ in repentance and faith, depending upon the promises of God and looking forward to a future inheritance.

Two Cities

Cain was building a city (Gen. 4:17). Outwardly you could say that he was prospering. In the eyes of this world, Cain was making progress and achieving great things.

Like many of us, Cain felt that he needed security. After Cain killed his brother, God drove him from his presence and condemned him to a fugitive life. But to help Cain when he was afraid of suffering Abel's fate, God had graciously marked him for protection. Yet despite God's kindness, Cain took matters into his own hands. What does this tell us about Cain and what he was building?

Cain was working extremely hard to establish himself on earth. His thoughts and energy were centred on this life. He craved family honour and named a city after his son. And he was doing all this in a time of great social change. Notice all the firsts that you can see in these verses: the first man to farm in a scientific way; the beginning of music and the arts; and progress in metal work and technology. This was an enterprising and successful community. But they were living without God. Cain had walked out of God's presence and was working for himself.

Even today, men and women are struggling and working hard to make it here on earth. If I get a good job, people say to themselves, if I find a wife/husband, if I am living comfortably, then I will be happy and content. This is the way of Cain and we must beware of it. Things may look good outwardly, but spiritually we may be in great danger. Cain's story demonstrates to us that having a city or a big house is not evidence that a person is right with God. What is important is spiritual wealth which comes through a radical change in our innermost being. This is how the Lord Jesus put it: "you must be born again" (John 3:7).

Cain's city was built for man's glory. His misplaced zeal to establish his name on earth finds echoes down the ages up to our own materialistic era. Work, possessions, entertainment, fame; this, our world assures us, is the path to fulfilment. These are the materials of which our cities are built. And it is man's glory that inspires us to build them. But the way of Cain leads to destruction because "Unless the LORD builds the house, those who build it labour in vain. Unless the LORD watches over the city, the watchman stays awake in vain" (Ps. 127:1).

But God is building a different city; a city that is for his glory. Those who love him are looking forward to this heavenly city. We read of the heroes of the faith that "they desire a better country, that is, a heavenly one. Therefore God is not ashamed to be called their God, for he has prepared for them a city" (Heb. 11:16). The reality is that "here we have no lasting city, but we seek the city that is to come" (Heb. 13:14). Paul wrote: "But our citizenship is in heaven, and from it we await a Saviour, the Lord Jesus Christ" (Phil. 3:20).

It is tragic that many preachers are no longer preaching about this heavenly city. Instead, they are busy turning our eyes to Cain's worldly city. They no longer preach about the Christian's sure and certain hope, which is an "inheritance that is imperishable, undefiled, and unfading, kept in heaven for you" (1 Pet. 1:4). Instead they motivate people to pursue worldly success, happiness, and fulfilment in this short life.

My fellow preacher, there are two cities. Which one are you preaching? My fellow believer, which city are you wholeheartedly pursuing?

The city of Cain was not abiding; it did not last. Some commentators even suggest that Cain never finished building it. Those who seek fulfillment in the things that this world offers will only be disappointed in the end. They will find themselves alienated from God for all eternity.

But the family of Seth called upon the name of the Lord. They knew true prosperity, they believed in God's promises, and they looked forward to the eternal, heavenly city. True believers rest on the hope of eternal life with God and they will not be disappointed.

Polygamy is Not Prosperity

The story of Cain and his family has another warning for us. It was a descendant of Cain, Lamech[i], who introduced polygamy into the world. Some people today see polygamy as a mark of prosperity. In Africa, having many wives can be associated with wealth, power, and fame. When I was a young boy, if I saw a man marrying another wife, I knew that he had been promoted at his place of work. A man with only one wife used to be referred to as having one eye. Recently, one African leader married a fifth wife and there was dancing and celebration in that ceremony. We have seen men parading their wives to show others how prosperous and mighty they are. There is even a preacher who said that God appeared to him and told him to marry another wife; he is now advocating polygamy.

However, in Genesis 4:19 we see that it was Lamech, a godless descendant of Cain, who first corrupted the institution of marriage with polygamy. Genesis 2:24 clearly teaches us that only one man and one woman should become one flesh. Lamech violated the clear instruction given by God. Since God created marriage to be between one man and one woman (Matt. 19:4-5), polygamy is not a sign of prosperity as our culture wants us to believe; it is a sin. If you are married to one wife, it is God's will for you to be faithful to her. If you are considering marriage, I plead with you in the name of the Lord, do not follow the way of Lamech.

Some of you are already polygamists and I urge you to come to the Lord just as you are, for the Bible says

---

i   This is a different Lamech from the one who was descended from Seth and was the father of Noah.

that "each one should remain in the condition in which he was called" (1 Cor. 7:20). You should not abandon any of your wives. Some churches wrongly deny polygamists church membership and the Lord's Supper. However, polygamists should not become church leaders (1 Tim. 3:2). Those who are saved and in the church should not abandon those they have married before they were saved, but they also must not promote polygamy in any way.

Polygamy is not prosperity, but a transgression of God's law, and the Bible makes clear its consequences. Many wives turned Solomon's heart from the Lord (1 Kings 11:4). Polygamy caused Rebecca and Isaac grief (Gen. 26:35); it caused jealousy between wives (Gen. 30:1, 1 Sam. 1:6); and trouble between children (Gen. 37, Judg. 9). I come from a polygamous family and I understand this well. When the father of the family dies, even before the burial, arguments and rivalry can pull the family apart. Polygamy is not prosperity.

Do Not Envy the Godless

Cain and his descendants would certainly be regarded as successful today: property, cultural sophistication, technology, and multiple wives. The logic of the prosperity gospel leads many to wrongly assume that the modern day equivalents of Cain's family are blessed. But even for believers who refuse to base their hope on worldly possessions, there are still temptations to overcome. Envy constantly distracts us from the single-minded pursuit of God's city.

We look at the prosperity and achievements of godless people and are perplexed like the psalmist: "But as for me, my feet had almost stumbled, my steps had nearly slipped. For I was envious of the arrogant when I saw the prosperity of the wicked" (Ps. 73:2-3). The psalmist then lists some characteristics, similar to those we saw in Cain's family, which modern prosperity gospel preachers are now exalting. The wicked, he writes, appear to have no struggles, their bodies are healthy and strong, they are proud and at ease, and they increase in riches.

But while the Bible recognizes how we are tempted, it also opens our eyes to help us fight temptation. God showed the psalmist that rich people who are arrogant and uncaring are standing on the edge of the abyss. The destiny of these people is destruction (Ps. 73:17-20) and we need to pity and warn them rather than envy them. The presence and wisdom of God changed the psalmist's perspective on the godlessly prosperous. We must think and live in the light of eternity.

The descendants of Cain were not known for their worship but for their worldly achievements and prosperity. They did not know God and their accomplishments could not cover their rejection of the one they needed the most. Of course, material things are not necessarily bad. But if we live for material prosperity and success, then we are building our house on sand. The descendants of Cain were on slippery ground and their destiny was judgement. They thought that they had achieved so much, but they had built nothing that could last.

God has declared to his people: "And do you seek great things for yourself? Seek them not" (Jer. 45:5). He repeatedly warned the children of Israel not to boast about their wisdom, strength, and wealth (Jer. 9:23). And yet today's prosperity preachers want us to live for these very things. We see over and over again that the most important thing in life is having an intimate and right relationship with

God. As God has declared, "let him who boasts boast in this: that he understands and knows me" (Jer. 9:24).

True Prosperity

But what exactly does this spiritual prosperity, which God wants us to seek, look like? After showing us the bad example of Cain's family, Genesis 4 points us in the right direction: "At that time people began to call on the name of the LORD" (Gen. 4:26). For these early believers, God was where he belonged—at the centre of their lives. They trusted, sought, and worshipped God. And worshipping God is what man was made for; as the Westminster Shorter Catechism puts it, "Man's chief end is to glorify God and to enjoy him forever."

From the descendants of Seth to the early Christians, God's people have distinguished themselves as worshippers. God's people are separate from the world because God's name, honour, glory, and reputation thrill them more than anything this world can offer. Seth's family worshipped the promise giver and promise keeper; the one who had promised a Saviour. Christians today worship the same faithful God; the one who has kept his promise and sent the Lord Jesus Christ. They believe in the promises of God and look forward with great joy to the return of the Lord Jesus Christ and to the new heavens and the new earth.

The prosperity gospel distracts people from the God-centred truth of the gospel. It diverts their focus away from the death of the Lord Jesus at Calvary. It distracts from the substitutionary atonement, the crucified life, and holiness. It obscures the great future hope of Christ's return and the age to come when we will be with him.

God does not save us primarily to bless us with material things, but to change us to be like Christ. Paul writes: "Do not be conformed to this world, but be transformed by the renewal of your mind" (Rom. 12:2). The Christian church throughout the ages has recognized that the atonement, which the Lord Jesus accomplished on the cross of Calvary, is the central theme of the Christian message (Isa. 53:5, John 1:29, 2 Cor. 5:21, 1 John 4:10). But this is contrary to what we are hearing today when the central theme is man and what God can do for him. Even singing is dominated by 'God-bless-me' choruses. We need to go back to the central message of the Bible. Those who know the Lord and worship him as the centre of their lives have true prosperity.

Spiritual Prosperity above Temporary Prosperity

The consequences of embracing false prosperity are deadly to our faith. Once we have removed God from the centre, and replaced him with material things, other errors quickly follow. Firstly, we forget the source of all blessing. And, secondly, we lose the reality that, even on this earth, spiritual blessings are infinitely superior to material ones. The Apostle Paul helps us correct these errors: "Blessed be the God and Father of our Lord Jesus Christ, who has blessed us in Christ with every spiritual blessing in the heavenly places" (Eph. 1:3). These spiritual blessings come from God. They do not come from bishops, reverends, pastors, or churches.

Many prosperity gospel preachers even want us to believe that blessings come from anointing oil, falling backward, or holy water. Some have now gone as far as

selling brooms and salt with which, they claim, demons
are swept away and Christians preserved from attacks.
But the Bible tells us clearly that our blessings come from
God.

But, you may ask, how do we receive these blessings?
How does God deliver his blessings to us? Again, Ephesians 1:3 gives us the answer. They are received in and
through Christ alone. All the blessings from God the Father reach us through Christ. Do not let people fool you
into believing that they have power in themselves to bless
others.

Just as Seth and his descendants paid more attention
to spiritual things than external achievements, the Apostle Paul assures us that God has blessed his people with
every spiritual blessing. The blessings are called spiritual
because they are from God and invisible to man's eyes.
They do not primarily concern our outward circumstances here in this world. They are eternal. Paul shows us that
the blessings we already have in Christ, which Christ won
for all God's people, are of greater value than any material
thing we could possess:

> *Even as he chose us* in him *before the foundation
> of the world, that we should be holy and blameless
> before him. In love he predestined us for adoption
> as sons* through Jesus Christ, *according to the pur-
> pose of his will, to the praise of his glorious grace,
> with which he has blessed us* in the Beloved. In him
> *we have redemption through his blood, the forgive-
> ness of our trespasses, according to the riches of
> his grace, which he lavished upon us, in all wisdom
> and insight making known to us the mystery of his
> will, according to his purpose, which he set forth* in

Christ *as a plan for the fullness of time, to unite all things* in him, *things in heaven and things on earth.*

In him *we have obtained an inheritance, having been predestined according to the purpose of him who works all things according to the counsel of his will, so that we who were the first to hope in Christ might be to the praise of his glory. In him you also, when you heard the word of truth, the gospel of your salvation, and believed in him, were sealed with the promised Holy Spirit, who is the guarantee of our inheritance until we acquire possession of it, to the praise of his glory. (Eph. 1:4-14)*

Look at the list of a Christian's wonderful spiritual blessings: chosen, predestined, loved, adopted, accepted, redeemed, enlightened, forgiven, and sealed by the Holy Spirit to guarantee a divine inheritance. These are everlasting blessings that cannot be destroyed and, therefore, can also provide more joy, purer delight, and firmer contentment now than any of the temporary blessings in which we are urged by prosperity preachers to place our hope.

God's people possess a joy and contentment that is beyond the reach of the difficulty and sadness we experience. If you are a married couple without children, let no one look down on you. You are blessed and your marriage is complete with or without children. If you are born again, born of God, you have been richly blessed whether you are living in a thatched house or in a mansion. A man may live in material poverty his whole life and yet be better off than a rich businessman because his treasure is in heaven where moth and rust do not destroy (Matt. 6:19). A Christian woman may endure an illness for many years and yet that suffering cannot rob her of the blessings of Ephesians 1 and she can savour the promise of heaven where there will be no more crying or pain (Rev. 21:4). You may be persecuted, but Jesus said you are blessed because the kingdom of heaven is yours (Matt. 5:10).

Prayer and Prosperity

We have seen that God consistently warns us not to focus on temporary honour and blessings that only last as long as this life. And just as firmly, God points us toward the God-centred, eternal blessings that God has promised and given us in Jesus Christ. How can we gauge where we stand in this struggle? Are there warning signs that we are abandoning the prosperity that comes from God in exchange for this world's inferior substitute? According to Jesus, how we pray indicates our priorities and our relationship with God.

The prosperity gospel has changed the way people pray. Many prayers today are focused on earthly rather than spiritual things – you just need to switch on your radio or TV and you will hear the evidence. Often these materialistic prayers are based on Bible verses which have been taken completely out of context. If you pray for spiritual things today, you may even find that some church members will start complaining. So how should we pray? In Colossians we see that priority is given to spiritual prosperity:

And so, from the day we heard, we have not ceased to pray for you, asking that you may be filled with the knowledge of his will in all spiritual wisdom

and understanding, so as to walk in a manner
worthy of the Lord, fully pleasing to him, bearing
fruit in every good work and increasing in the
knowledge of God. May you be strengthened with
all power, according to his glorious might, for all
endurance and patience with joy, giving thanks to
the Father, who has qualified you to share in the
inheritance of the saints in light. He has delivered
us from the domain of darkness and transferred
us to the kingdom of his beloved Son, in whom we
have redemption, the forgiveness of sins. (Col. 1:9-
14)

What does Paul pray for the Colossian Christians?
Paul does not pray that they may be materially wealthy;
he does not pray that they may be successful in business;
he does not pray that they may buy a better house; he does
not pray that they always be healthy; he does not pray that
they will not die. Instead, he prays that God will fill them
with the knowledge of his will through spiritual wisdom
and understanding.

He prays this in order that they may live a life worthy of
the Lord and please him in every way. And Paul shows us
what it means to live a life worthy of the Lord, which is in
contrast to what the prosperity preachers focus on. A life
worthy of the Lord is a life of bearing fruit in every good
work, growing in the knowledge of God, being strengthened by God's power to endure, and joyfully giving thanks
to the Father. Is this how you pray for others and yourself? Or when you pray are you only concentrating on
promotions, cars, and comfort? We may and should pray
for our physical needs (Luke 11:3), but such prayers must
not push out or dominate prayers for our spiritual needs

and the kingdom of God (Luke 11:2-4). Our prayers must give priority to spiritual things.

Conclusion: The Great Division

Since the fall there has been a great division: those who reject God, like Cain, and those who call on the name of the Lord, like Seth. There is a divide between those who store up, and live for, treasures in this life, and those who store up treasures in heaven. The clash between these two sides is not new; but as the prosperity gospel spreads through our churches, we must confront it with the wisdom of God in the clear teaching of the Bible.

When we are bombarded with the false prosperity of worldliness, we need to hold on to the true prosperity of godliness. We must *reject* Cain's city which exists for the glory of man and is heading for oblivion, *in order to seek* the better, heavenly, and eternal city that God has prepared for his people. As part of this, God calls us to turn away from the sin of polygamy and embrace marriage as God has created it – one man and one woman. And while the fleeting benefits of Cain's city sometimes cause us to envy, God draws our attention to the bigger picture; the godlessly prosperous are destined for destruction.

True prosperity is enjoyed by those whose focus is God. In all ages, God's people have been defined, distinguished, and blessed by their worship of him. Their worship is filled with the knowledge that God alone is the source of all blessing in and through Jesus Christ. And it is deepened by the truth that the spiritual blessings God gives his people are secure from anything or anyone in this world. This is why their prayers are dominated by spiritual desires. We live in a materialistic world, but God calls his people to something better by far.

CHAPTER 3

The Gospel Life

Kenneth Mbugua

"Enter by the narrow gate. For the gate is wide and the way is easy that leads to destruction, and those who enter by it are many. For the gate is narrow and the way is hard that leads to life, and those who find it are few. Beware of false prophets, who come to you in sheep's clothing but inwardly are ravenous wolves. You will recognize them by their fruits. Are grapes gathered from thornbushes, or figs from thistles? So, every healthy tree bears good fruit, but the diseased tree bears bad fruit. A healthy tree cannot bear bad fruit, nor can a diseased tree bear good fruit. Every tree that does not bear good fruit is cut down and thrown into the fire. Thus you will recognize them by their fruits. Not everyone who says to me, 'Lord, Lord,' will enter the kingdom of heaven, but the one who does the will of my Father who is in heaven." (Matthew 7:13-21)

Back when they did not have machines to identify fake currency, banks used to teach their tellers to get used to the feel of real money in their hands. The idea was that the best way to recognise a fake is to intimately know the real thing. We intend to follow this method. Spending time with the gospel in God's word means that when we encounter a fake gospel, we can see it for what it is.

We are going to look at the life of Christ, the apostles, and also select figures in church history to see if the lives of our forefathers in the gospel match up with the message of the prosperity gospel and the lifestyle that its preachers advocate. This will equip us with the knowledge we need to sniff out false gospels and wayward teachers.

The lifestyle of many preachers of the prosperity gospel is defined by affluence and extravagance. And they preach that God intends for all Christians to live like they do. As theologian and pastor Gordon Fee explains, while this error springs from wrong interpretation of the Bible, its manifestation is a materialistic life defended with this repeated false affirmation:

> God wills the financial prosperity of every one of his children, and therefore for a Christian to be in poverty is to be outside of God's intended will; it is to be living a Satan defeated life. And usually tucked away with this affirmation is a second: Because we are God's children (the King's kids, as some like to put it) we should always go first class - we should always have the biggest and the best,

a Cadillac instead of a Volkswagen, because this
alone brings glory to God.[i]

Does this central premise of the prosperity gospel
stand in the light of scripture? Does the Bible teach us
that because we are God's children, we should always
have the best of this world? What do the examples of our
Lord and his disciples show us we should seek in this life?

Jesus Christ

The Bible teaches us that Jesus Christ was one of the
wealthiest people in his day. He lived in a big mansion on
the Mount of Olives and had a whole host of servants to do
his bidding at the snap of his fingers. As he was the Son of
God, he obviously never knew suffering or pain. Everyone
loved him because God even made his enemies become
his friends. When he went to the synagogues, he focused
on material prosperity and the good life that people could
have now. The Bible also tells us that he promised all who
would follow him to expect a trouble-free life like his own.
Right?

The gospels inform us that this is the *opposite of reality*. Christ lived a life marked with struggle and pain.
We will take some time to look at texts which describe
that life. The truth about Jesus' life and mission in these
verses is largely self-evident. We seek to expose you to it
and allow your familiarity with that truth to equip you to
compare and contrast it with the examples and teachings
of prosperity gospel preachers.

---

i   Gordon Fee, *The Disease of the Health and Wealth Gospels* (Regent College Publishing: Vancouver, 2006), 8.

What kind of life did the Son of God lead on earth and what does it tell us about the life his followers should expect for themselves? In Matthew 10:24-25 Christ assured those who followed him that they should expect a life like his:

> *A disciple is not above his teacher, nor a servant above his master. It is enough for the disciple to be like his teacher, and the servant like his master. If they have called the master of the house Beelzebul, how much more will they malign those of his household? (Matt. 10:24-25)*

Using the clear principle that a servant is not above his master, Christ shows us that if the master suffered, the servant should expect nothing less. If the master was called a devil, the servants should expect the same and worse. As we look at the life of the master, it will become evident that some supposed servants are seeking to be more than their master.

Let us start with his home background. Luke 2 gives us a hint about the social status of Jesus' earthly parents. When they went to the Temple, they offered a sacrifice for the birth of the first male of their household that was reserved for those who could not afford a lamb.

> *And when the time came for their purification according to the Law of Moses, they brought him up to Jerusalem to present him to the Lord ... to offer a sacrifice according to what is said in the Law of the Lord, "a pair of turtledoves, or two young pigeons." (Luke 2:22, 24)*

As Mary and Joseph could not afford a lamb for such an important sacrifice, it is safe to assume that there were many things they could not afford as Jesus grew up; the same Jesus who was born in a manger surrounded by the smell of animals. If a modest upbringing was good enough for the Son of God, are we not misguided to preach that, as children of God, we should expect to live a first class life here on earth? A servant is not above his master.

But maybe that was just his upbringing. Perhaps when he grew up he left his humble start far behind and started enjoying the highlife. Did Jesus show us the archetypal rags to riches story of small beginnings leading to material prosperity? Luke 9 suggests otherwise. When a local scribe volunteered to become one of Christ's disciples, Jesus outlined the terms and conditions: "Foxes have holes, and birds of the air have nests, but the Son of Man has nowhere to lay his head" (Luke 9:58). Christ did not live in a mansion on a hill as some today would like to think. He was content with the minimum he needed. As his apostle later wrote, "if we have food and clothing, with these we will be content" (1 Tim. 6:8). If poverty was enough for the master, should the servants demand more?

Ultimately, the cross defines Christ's life. He was born to die. God the Father ordained his life to be one of suffering. If you try to explain Christ's life without focusing on the suffering that he came to endure on our behalf, you end up with an ungodly fiction. Isaiah's messianic prophecy captures Jesus Christ's life for us in these words:

He was despised and rejected by men; a man of sorrows, and acquainted with grief; and as one from whom men hide their faces he was despised, and we esteemed him not. Surely he has borne our

griefs and carried our sorrows; yet we esteemed
him stricken, smitten by God, and afflicted. But he
was pierced for our transgressions; he was crushed
for our iniquities; upon him was the chastisement
that brought us peace, and with his wounds we are
healed. (Isa. 53:3-5)

Jesus' mission as messiah was filled with pain and
suffering: despised, rejected, man of sorrows, acquainted
with grief, not esteemed, stricken, smitten by God, afflicted, pierced, crushed, and wounded.[ii] The call to follow
this Lord is not a call to walk an easy road. Isaac Watts
summarised the difference between the Christian's path
and our selfish demands, when he wrote: "Must I be carried to the skies on flowery beds of ease? While others
fought to win the prize and sailed through bloody seas?"[iii]
Our Lord who suffered for us called us to be ready to
do the same. "Whoever does not bear his own cross and
come after me cannot be my disciple" (Luke 14:27). To
follow Christ is to be ready to accept pain and suffering.
While Jesus showed us—and prepared us for—a simple and hard life, he also made it clear that we should not
even *want* to be rich. "Take care, and be on your guard
against all covetousness, for one's life does not consist
in the abundance of his possessions" (Luke 12:15). Jesus
Christ warned that the pursuit of wealth was not a godly
quest but a grave danger to avoid. When he taught his
disciples about wealth, he did not teach them secrets of

---

ii   If you have been taught that this text means that Christ's poverty
and suffering has bought us a life now in which we will not suffer,
please read Chapter 1 on misinterpretations of the Bible.

iii This is from the hymn *Am I a Soldier of the Cross* by Isaac Watts.

how to attain it. Instead, he told them to let go of loving it. Letting go of the lust for money is a must if you want to take hold of Jesus (Luke 16:13).

Jesus lived a simple and humble life. And he taught us to beware of the allure of getting rich. He said that his people should expect suffering and not judge their life according to the material things that they possessed. Now look at the life and doctrine of prosperity gospel preachers. Are they preaching Jesus' message? Does the lifestyle they commend look like the life that Jesus lived and preached?

The Apostles

If the prosperity gospel is true, then we would expect those who were the gospel's original witnesses and preachers to teach and manifest this message more than anyone else. Today's famous exponents of the prosperity gospel live in mansions, own fleets of luxurious cars, and travel in personal jets. Those not as famous seek to attain those heights and in the meantime make a great show of their prosperity. But look at the lives of the apostles. You will see a sharp contrast; a contrast that exposes so-called modern apostles as preachers of a counterfeit gospel.

The example of the apostles is that worldly benefits are not important. This is how Paul defined the lives of the apostles:

> For I think that God has exhibited us apostles as last of all, like men sentenced to death, because we have become a spectacle to the world, to angels, and to men. We are fools for Christ's sake, but you are wise in Christ. We are weak, but you are

strong. You are held in honour, but we in disre-
pute. To the present hour we hunger and thirst, we
are poorly dressed and buffeted and homeless, and
we labour, working with our own hands. When
reviled, we bless; when persecuted, we endure;
when slandered, we entreat. We have become, and
are still, like the scum of the world, the refuse of all
things. (1 Cor. 4:9-13)

Paul wrote this to Christians who thought too highly of themselves in order to rebuke them. He drew a valuable contrast between their conceit and the apostles' godly lowliness.

Suffering was fundamental to Paul's understanding of serving God. Four times in his second letter to Timothy, Paul taught his spiritual son to be ready to suffer. Instead of running away from suffering, Paul said that we should "share in suffering for the gospel by the power of God" (2 Tim. 1:8). "Share in suffering," Paul emphasised later, not as an exception, but "as a good soldier of Christ Jesus" (2 Tim. 2:3). And just in case we wanted to escape the universal nature of his message, Paul stated that "all who desire to live a godly life in Christ Jesus will be persecuted" (2 Tim. 3:12).

Living a godly life means embracing suffering, not avoiding it. Could there be a clearer contrast with health and wealth teaching? Paul showed Timothy and reminds us (as Jesus Christ did before him) that we should expect suffering as a natural result of being a Christian. "As for you, always be sober-minded, endure suffering, do the work of an evangelist, fulfil your ministry" (2 Tim. 4:5). Suffering is an essential part of being a follower of Jesus Christ.

When we understand this, we do not need to be ashamed of suffering. Look at Paul's litany of pain:

Five times I received at the hands of the Jews the forty lashes less one. Three times I was beaten with rods. Once I was stoned. Three times I was shipwrecked; a night and a day I was adrift at sea; on frequent journeys, in danger from rivers, danger from robbers, danger from my own people, danger from Gentiles, danger in the city, danger in the wilderness, danger at sea, danger from false brothers; in toil and hardship, through many a sleepless night, in hunger and thirst, often without food, in cold and exposure. (2 Cor. 11:24-27)

Do not miss the reason why Paul is recounting these experiences. When you look at the context, you see that Paul wrote this as evidence that he was a servant of Christ. His scars bore testimony to his authenticity as an apostle of his suffering saviour. When prosperity preachers offer wealth as proof of their faithfulness, think about Paul who did the opposite. "For the sake of Christ, then," Paul concluded, "I am content with weaknesses, insults, hardships, persecutions, and calamities. For when I am weak, then I am strong" (2 Cor. 12:10). Humble Christians redirect attention to their glorious God. They are content with suffering because it glorifies the riches of God's grace.

Why is there so much attention given to suffering in the New Testament? None of Paul's difficulties came as a surprise to him and God does not want them to come as a surprise to us. If Christians understand that suffering is normal for a faithful Christian, then pain cannot shake their faith. When Christ called Paul to himself, he wanted him to know the cost at the beginning: "For I will show him how much he must suffer for the sake of my name" (Acts 9:16). Studying the lives of the apostles helps us be ready for trouble and know that God's blessing is in it.

Paul was not the exception. James was executed by order of Herod (Acts 12:2). Peter was imprisoned (Acts 12:3) and church tradition suggests that later he was crucified – a cruel death for which Christ had prepared him (John 21:18-19). The Apostles were beaten for preaching (Acts 5:40-41) and Stephen was stoned to death (Acts 7:54-58). And Paul himself, before his conversion, distinguished himself by his eager attacks on those who claimed Jesus as Lord (Acts 8:3). The apostles and first Christians suffered and died for Jesus.

The Bible's testimony of the apostles does not square with the teachings of the prosperity gospel. These servants of Christ, of whom the world was not worthy, did not lead first class lives here on earth and they did not expect to. They followed Christ knowing that suffering and pain was not a possibility but a guarantee. And in doing so they demonstrated the lineage of faith that reaches back to Moses who "considered the reproach of Christ greater wealth than the treasures of Egypt, for he was looking to the reward" (Heb. 11:26). Sufferings in and for Christ are greater riches than any prosperity we could ever possess in this world.

The Persecuted Church

We have seen the grief and sorrow of our Lord and the suffering of the pioneering apostles as they built on the foundations that Christ had established. Consider even the example of God's most faithful servants *before* Christ?

Some were tortured, refusing to accept release, so that they might rise again to a better life. Others suffered mocking and flogging, and even chains and imprisonment. They were stoned, they were sawn in two, they were killed with the sword. They went about in skins of sheep and goats, destitute, afflicted, mistreated—of whom the world was not worthy—wandering about in deserts and mountains, and in dens and caves of the earth. (Heb. 11:35-38)

But is that all in the past? Did it take place so that future generations could live in ease? Is luxury and comfort the subsequent manifestation of the work and presence of God? Church history answers those questions decisively. The spread of the gospel and the sanctification of Christians have always been marked by suffering.

In this section we will take a few examples from church history of believers who demonstrate the presence of God in the suffering of his people for their faith. There are many sources that can give you information about persecuted Christians both past and present. *Foxe's Book of Martyrs* is a historical compilation that we will make use of in this section. Look also at the websites of organizations such as Voice of the Martyrs (*www.persecution.com*) and International Christian Concern (*www.persecution.org*) to find many accounts of Christians who are suffering *now* for Christ all over the world.

Many faithful Christians are dying for Jesus Christ; brothers and sisters whose lives and deaths bring great glory to God as they affirm Paul's creed: "to live is Christ, and to die is gain" (Phil. 1:21). What mockery against these saints to preach that Christians should not suffer!

This is to preach that the apostles, the early church, and the persecuted church through the years suffered in vain. On the contrary, these Christians are the best expressions of the spirit of Christ. We need to learn from their lives.

Let us begin with one of the early church fathers, Polycarp. He was the bishop of Smyrna in the second century AD. Here is an account of the conclusion of his trial by the Roman authorities in which he had been charged with being a follower of Christ:

> *The proconsul then urged him, saying, "Swear, and I will release thee; reproach Christ." Polycarp answered, "Eighty and six years have I served him, and he never once wronged me; how then shall I blaspheme my King, Who hath saved me?"[iv]*

This great Christian submitted calmly to his execution rather than betray Christ. The history of the Roman Empire contains numerous similar accounts. For example, seventy years later, in Rome itself, there was a woman named Cecilia. She gave up the comforts of a respectable family, not only believing in Christ but passionately bringing others to him, even if it killed her.

> *She converted her husband and brother, who were beheaded; and the maximus, or officer, who led them to execution, becoming their convert, suffered the same fate. The lady was placed naked in a scalding bath, and having continued there a*

---

iv   John Foxe, *Foxe's Book of Martyrs* (Peabody: Hendrickson, 2004), 14.

considerable time, her head was struck off with a sword, A.D. 222.[v]

Faithful Christians suffered gruesome punishments for Jesus in our own beloved Africa. "Saturninus, a priest of Albitina, a town of Africa, after being tortured, was remanded to prison, and there starved to death. His four children, after being variously tormented, shared the same fate with their father."[vi] We could go on indefinitely with the testimonies of Christians dying for Christ through the years and across the globe. This historical record demands a response from us. Were these saints wrong to suffer for the gospel?

As you read this, many of your brothers and sisters are suffering persecution because of their faith in Christ. For millions of Christians in Asia, Nigeria, Sudan, and many Islamic states, death for the sake of faithfulness to Christ is a real prospect. In fact, Islamic terrorism has brought the possibility of martyrdom for Christ to any street in the world. Think of the Christians singled out and brutally murdered at Garissa University College in Kenya recently. It was chilling to hear of brothers and sisters gunned down by evil men as they gathered for prayer. But as we long for the day when such horror will be no more, let us not dishonour these Christian martyrs by forgetting that they have gained immeasurably more than they lost.

The author of Hebrews wrote this about such men and women:

---

v   Ibid., 19.
vi Ibid., 36.

These all died in faith, not having received the things promised, but having seen them and greeted them from afar, and having acknowledged that they were strangers and exiles on the earth. For people who speak thus make it clear that they are seeking a homeland. If they had been thinking of that land from which they had gone out, they would have had opportunity to return. But as it is, they desire a better country, that is, a heavenly one. Therefore God is not ashamed to be called their God, for he has prepared for them a city. (Heb. 11:13-16)

What kind of teaching prepares ordinary people to take such a stand and meet such an end? Prosperity preaching leaves Christians unable to make sense of the central place of suffering in the lives of those who follow Christ. It leaves men and women unequipped and confused in the face of poverty and pain. Only the genuine hope and glory of the gospel of Jesus Christ enables Christians to understand persecution and pain now. As a twentieth century martyr for the gospel, Jim Elliot, famously said: "He is no fool who gives what he cannot keep to gain that which he cannot lose."

Conclusion

Think about the examples of Jesus Christ, the apostles, and suffering Christians through the centuries. Then look at the example and message of the prosperity gospel preachers. We have the genuine currency of Christ's gos-

pel and its servants before us; we can, therefore, identify
and reject the worthless counterfeit gospel of health and
wealth.

CHAPTER 4

Suffering

Kenneth Mbugua

So we do not lose heart. Though our outer self is wasting away, our inner self is being renewed day by day. For this light momentary affliction is preparing for us an eternal weight of glory beyond all comparison, as we look not to the things that are seen but to the things that are unseen. For the things that are seen are transient, but the things that are unseen are eternal. (2 Corinthians 4:16-18)

We live in a world full of suffering. Earthquakes, hurricanes, drought, famine, and war destroy lives, homes, communities, and nations. On a personal level, who is not familiar with the pain of rejection, betrayal, and conflict? Daily we are vulnerable to the threat of sudden suffering – accidents can bring us loss and grief in a moment. And we live exposed to the pain of disease that can slowly or quickly take our lives and the lives of those we love. Is there any doubt that we live in a broken world?

Ever since suffering entered the world, we have been trying to escape it. There are few quests more natural for humans than avoiding pain and increasing pleasure. We invent new machines and strategies all with the implicit promise: more pleasure, less pain. We pursue better jobs, more money, and better health. We search for better relationships, greater churches, and more inspirational pastors. Our pursuit of more joy and less suffering is at the root of so much of human activity. Does the Bible condemn this search? No, but it corrects our understanding of suffering and provides us the only road to joy, through suffering.

Prosperity preaching is popular because it taps into this most basic of human desires. But it offers a solution to suffering that is unbiblical, misleading and, ultimately, detrimental to those who follow it. And rather than saving people, this false solution leaves many discouraged, disillusioned, and bitter with God and his people. The prosperity gospel is not the solution God has given for our suffering; it is not the good news. In this chapter we will look specifically at what God teaches us about suffering and how it contradicts the alluring but fraudulent escape of the prosperity gospel.

Understanding Suffering

There are three basic questions that African herders would ask if they found a cow trapped in a ditch: How did the cow end up there? How can we get it out? And how can we keep the cow from going back into the ditch? Similarly, in order to understand the solution that God provides for the problem of suffering, we have to understand why suffering exists, the only way to deal with it, and how it can be kept from recurring.

There was a time when there was no suffering, but it was sin—our rejection of God—that brought pain into this world. And in the future, there will be a new age in which there will again be no suffering. What bridges this divide? Christ came to deal with our sin and all its consequences by dying on the cross, defeating death in resurrection, and ascending to heaven. His physical and spiritual suffering on the cross for us has fully paid the penalty for our sin, purchasing our complete redemption along with the restoration of creation. His blood has achieved everything necessary for the formation of a new heaven and a new earth, eternally free from suffering (Rom. 8:18-25).

If we do not understand why suffering exists, what God has done about it, and what that means for us, we will be vulnerable to false solutions. At great cost, God has provided an everlasting solution to our problem of sin and its painful consequences. But this good news has been seriously marred and distorted by preachers of the prosperity gospel.

The Genesis of Suffering

The first chapters of the Bible tell us that God made all things out of nothing. He was the originator, designer, and builder. And what he made was *very* good (Gen. 1:31). That original goodness included God's creation of mankind. Man and woman were at peace with God, each other, and the rest of creation. Everything was good until man decided that God was not enough.

In Genesis 3, Adam and Eve disobeyed God. He had told them: "You may surely eat of every tree of the garden, but of the tree of the knowledge of good and evil you shall not eat, for in the day that you eat of it you shall surely die" (Gen 2:16-17). God had clearly warned Adam and Eve that suffering would be the result if they chose to turn away from him. But, convinced by the serpent that satisfaction could be found outside of their relationship with God, they ignored God's warning and plunged into sin.

They reached out for more and found that it was less. They grabbed at wisdom and found that it was foolishness. And they searched for pleasure, but discovered pain. Suffering came into the world when man sought for pleasure and purpose outside God. Immediately after man and woman broke God's commandment, their world was shattered. They were afraid and ashamed - strange feelings that they had never felt before. This was the genesis of suffering: it came into the world through the doorway of sin.

Adam and Eve broke their communion with God and he soon explained to them some of the consequences.

> *To the woman he said, "I will surely multiply your pain in childbearing; in pain you shall bring forth children. Your desire shall be for your husband, and he shall rule over you." And to Adam he said, "Because you have listened to the voice of your wife and have eaten of the tree of which I commanded you, 'You shall not eat of it,' cursed is the ground because of you; in pain you shall eat of it all the days of your life; thorns and thistles it shall bring forth for you; and you shall eat the plants of the field. By the sweat of your face you shall eat bread,*

till you return to the ground, for out of it you were
taken; for you are dust, and to dust you shall re-
turn." (Gen. 3:16-19)

Look at the different aspects of suffering covered here.
There is intense physical pain. Relational struggles invade
the natural partnership of man and woman. The work
of life becomes a grinding toil. The land itself will share
man's corruption, fighting man's efforts to be productive.
And, worst of all, there is an end. With the sin of man
comes death.

What solution could there be for such a universal and
crushing curse? One of the problems of the prosperity
gospel's solution is that it is very similar to the cause of the
problem. Adam and Eve lacked satisfaction in what they
had in God, pursuing pleasure outside of their relationship with God and in addition to what he had promised.
Similarly, the prosperity gospel, instead of proclaiming
that God is more than enough, invites us to seek him in
order to attain additional material pleasures.

The source of pleasure in the prosperity gospel is not
God himself, but the things that God can get for us. But
just as Adam and Eve reached for pleasure and found
pain, the prosperity gospel's promises of fulfilment result
in emptiness. Why? Because they point us away from God
for satisfaction, just as the devil pointed the first man and
woman away from God. What they lost that day was their
relationship with God; and to be separated from him is
the definition of death. Reconciliation with God is what
Jesus calls life (John 17:3). You cannot solve the problem
of suffering by repeating the sin that caused it.

When Adam and Eve felt the sting of shame that their
sin had brought into the world, what did they do about

it? "Then the eyes of both were opened, and they knew that they were naked. And they sewed fig leaves together and made themselves loincloths" (Gen. 3:7). They tried to cover themselves with their own solution. And this is the flaw of the prosperity preachers; they offer us only worldly solutions. They point us to the same waterholes and broken cisterns that the world is seeking: jobs, houses, relationships, health, etc. (Jer. 2:13). We will seek the same waterholes, they tell us, but we will drink from them through God.

Do not be deceived. The prosperity gospel's worldly satisfactions are like Adam and Eve's fig leaves that temporarily covered their shame without dealing with it. The material solutions of man are unable to deal with the problems that man's ungodliness created. To properly deal with the problem of suffering, one has to deal with sin and alienation from God.

Even in Genesis 3 we can see God's solution to the problem of sin and its consequences. In the midst of the fall of man, the gospel emerged. God showed us in Genesis 3 that sacrifice, a substitute, and a saviour are what man needs to solve his problem of sin and suffering. As God cursed the serpent, he said: "I will put enmity between you and the woman, and between your offspring and her offspring; he shall bruise your head, and you shall bruise his heel" (Gen. 3:15). Since the early days of Christianity, God's people have understood this promise of Eve's ancestor crushing the serpent's head as the first prophecy of the messiah.

But in what way could man be saved by a messiah? "And the LORD God made for Adam and for his wife garments of skins and clothed them" (Gen. 3:21). It seems that God killed an animal so that this sacrificed beast could cover up the man and woman's shame, the result of their sin. Here we see the first sign of the biblical principle that the problem of sin is so great that it requires sacrificial atonement (Heb. 9:22). God would send his Son to be born and live as a man and to die as the sacrificial substitute, bearing the wrath of God at our sin on the cross for us. This is God's solution to the problem of sin and it is perfect. It is the only solution that will work.

God's solution deals with our suffering because it begins with its cause—sin. The solution to our suffering is not found in things that we get from God, it is found in being reconciled to God. In communion with God there is complete joy (Ps. 16:11); this is what sin had ruined and Christ has restored. But as we wait for our restoration to be completed in our resurrection bodies in the age to come, how can we understand the lingering consequences of sin that remain in this still broken world?

God's Promise of Restoration

God has reversed the curse. He justly cursed people because of their rebellion (Gen. 3:16-19) and the curse affects our bodies, relationships, vocations, and environment. But God's plan of restoration accomplished in Christ is as complete as the curse. The perfect plan of redemption and restoration is nearly finished and our faith in God to complete it can sustain us even when we suffer in this yet unredeemed and rebellious age.

Firstly, the coming restoration of our bodies gives joy to dying Christians: "For as in Adam all die, so also in Christ shall all be made alive" (1 Cor. 15:22). Paul revealed the nature of this restored body. "What is sown is perishable; what is raised is imperishable. It is sown in dishonour; it is raised in glory. It is sown in weakness; it is raised in power. It is sown a natural body; it is raised a spiritual body (1 Cor. 15:42-44). Before our bodies are restored, Christ serves as the prototype and the guarantee of our resurrection. Like him, in death we give up the temporary in order to gain the eternal.

Secondly, in Christ we can see the first signs of the restoration of our relationships with each other. Sin infects the bond of marriage with selfishness and jealousy. In the first family, brother even killed brother in envious rage. And so it has been since. But in Christ we can and should begin to replace pride with humility and serve each other (Phil. 2:1-4). When this happens, it is a sign of things to come. Our messiah is the Prince of *Peace* and his reign in the age to come will be defined by it (Isa. 9:6-7). So as we strive to live now in our saviour's peace rather than follow our contentious hearts, we hold on to the promises of God whose coming kingdom of peace will never end.

As well as promising peace in the Old Testament, God continually promised to restore Israel's fortune. For example, this was his promise through the prophet Amos:[i]

> *Behold, the days are coming ... when the plough-man shall overtake the reaper and the treader of grapes him who sows the seed; the mountains shall drip sweet wine, and all the hills shall flow with it. I will restore the fortunes of my people Israel, and they shall rebuild the ruined cities and inhabit them; they shall plant vineyards and drink*

i   Other examples: Ps. 14:7; Ps. 53:6; Jer. 30:3; Jer. 31:23; Jer. 33:7; Ezek. 39:25; Amos 19:14.

*their wine, and they shall make gardens and eat
their fruit. (Amos 9:13-14)*

This prophecy followed a frightening message of
judgement and gave its original hearers a real idea of how
God would restore his people. But the message is also for
God's people throughout history. A complete day of restoration is yet ahead. The struggles man has had in his work
shall one day be no more. Where he has known failure
and toil, he shall know success and pleasure. This is one
of the promises of the coming kingdom. When our best
efforts on earth seem to fail, we can remember that our
strife is temporary but our coming joyful fulfilment will
never end.

As part of God's plan of redemption, the whole creation
will be restored from its current corrupt state. The world
will be restored to a beauty that will even surpass that of
its original purity. And it is God's way that the restoration
of the creation follows from the salvation and freedom of
God's people in Christ.

*For the creation waits with eager longing for the
revealing of the sons of God. For the creation was
subjected to futility, not willingly, but because of
him who subjected it, in hope that the creation itself will be set free from its bondage to corruption
and obtain the freedom of the glory of the children
of God. (Rom. 8:19-21)*

Why is the Bible filled with God's promises to restore
and perfect our bodies, relationships, vocations, and environment? He knows that we need this sure hope, and
the signs we see of it now, to sustain us in the corruption

and sin that remains. God's solution to our struggle with suffering is the only ultimate and everlasting one. As we faithfully persevere through times of suffering, we begin to experience the blessings that will be ours in the age to come. In Christ's coming kingdom, we will thrive forever in his divine blessing and glory. God's solution is not temporary comfort, but an eternal plan that he has been working out since the beginning of time. God's people can see him continuing to unfold it and know that he will complete it – God's people and the world will be fully restored.

The Already Not Yet

As you can see, God's promises to his people are simultaneously present and future. Many prosperity gospel preachers use some of the verses above to 'prove' what Christians can have now. The error of their preaching is not in what Christians will receive, but when they will receive it. They change God's timeline and therefore distort God's plan of restoration.

When Paul wrote to the church in Corinth, he rebuked them for their misunderstanding of the blessings in Christ. "Already you have all you want! Already you have become rich! Without us you have become kings! And would that you did reign, so that we might share the rule with you!" (1 Cor. 4:8) Paul contrasted their arrogant attitude with the humility and poverty of the apostles. The Corinthian Christians were acting as if the blessings that God has promised for the world to come were already theirs.

If you are in Christ, then all God's promises are yours in him (2 Cor. 1:20). But as we live between the first and second comings of Jesus Christ, we still await the final consummation of God's plan and, therefore, the full blessings of being in Christ. When Paul writes about the glory that is ours in Christ, he looks to the future. He taught the Romans that "the sufferings of this present time are not worth comparing with the glory that is to be revealed to us" (Rom. 8:18). In case we miss the future orientation, he added: "For in this hope we were saved. Now hope that is seen is not hope. For who hopes for what he sees? But if we hope for what we do not see, we wait for it with patience" (Rom. 8:24-25). We will be free from all suffering in Christ; it is true. But we will receive this blessing at the end of this age and the completion of God's plan.

There are no ultimate solutions to our suffering in this world. But there is also no contradiction between our suffering now and our assurance that God will end all our suffering.

So we do not lose heart. Though our outer self is wasting away, our inner self is being renewed day by day. For this light momentary affliction is preparing for us an eternal weight of glory beyond all comparison, as we look not to the things that are seen but to the things that are unseen. For the things that are seen are transient, but the things that are unseen are eternal. (2 Cor. 4:16-18)

God's people endure suffering on this earth because they hold fast to the hope that God has put in them. They are justified, saved, and blessed now. And that assurance enables them to rejoice through suffering because they know that God will end all their suffering soon. The blessings of God now assure us of the much greater blessing that we do not have yet.

God's Purpose for Suffering

Therefore, the claim of the prosperity preachers that it is never God's will for us to suffer is repeatedly contradicted by the Bible. We must not allow people to be driven to fear and doubt by suffering because their preachers have not equipped them to make sense of it. Christians do not need to fear suffering not only because it will end, but because God is sovereign over it and uses it to bless his children.

We will look at this more in a later chapter, but let us now note a few reasons why suffering is not only temporary, but blessed. Firstly, God increases our faith in suffering. Peter, in explaining the future orientation of God's people, emphasized this:

> *According to his great mercy, he has caused us to be born again to a living hope through the resurrection of Jesus Christ from the dead, to an inheritance that is imperishable, undefiled, and unfading, kept in heaven for you, who by God's power are being guarded through faith for a salvation ready to be revealed in the last time. In this you rejoice, though now for a little while, if necessary, you have been grieved by various trials, so that the tested genuineness of your faith—more precious than gold that perishes though it is tested by fire—may be found to result in praise and glory and honour at the revelation of Jesus Christ. (1 Pet. 1:3-7)*

Do you see how the *everything-now* attitude of the prosperity gospel actually rejects the far greater wisdom of God's plan? As we persevere through suffering, looking to the future, it actually increases our faith in a way that glorifies God enduringly.

Christians are not exempt from suffering; they will definitely experience it and should *rejoice* in it. Look at what Peter went on to write:

Beloved, do not be surprised at the fiery trial when it comes upon you to test you, as though something strange were happening to you. But rejoice insofar as you share Christ's sufferings, that you may also rejoice and be glad when his glory is revealed. If you are insulted for the name of Christ, you are blessed, because the Spirit of glory and of God rests upon you. (1 Pet. 4:12-14)

To share in Jesus Christ's sufferings, as Paul understood, is to share in his resurrection and glory (Phil. 3:10). This is what Jesus had taught in the Sermon on the Mount (Matt. 5:10-12) and his disciples later put it into practice. After they had been flogged for preaching the gospel, they left "rejoicing that they were counted worthy to suffer dishonour for the name" (Acts 5:41). Freedom from suffering now is a false message that diverts Christians from God's plan and his blessing. Instead of following the prosperity gospel, we should follow God's word which encourages us: "Count it all joy, my brothers, when you meet trials of various kinds, for you know that the testing of your faith produces steadfastness. And let steadfastness have its full effect, that you may be perfect and complete, lacking in nothing" (James 1:2-4).

When prosperity preachers teach that it is never God's will for you to suffer, they undermine all the things that God can do in our lives through pain. He is in control of our temporary suffering in this world and he uses it to strengthen our faith. This suffering is so much a part of his good plan for us that God tells us to rejoice in it. When we suffer for God, we show our fellowship and partnership with Christ Jesus. That truly is a cause for joy and a gospel basis of sure hope.

Conclusion

We suffer in this world because of sin. Once we understand this, we must not look for solutions to suffering that avoid its root. God has a plan of redemption in which he has dealt with the problem of sin and its painful consequences forever. Jesus Christ bore the punishment we deserved for our sins when he suffered on the cross so we do not have to eternally suffer in hell.

God has reversed the curse and replaced it with restoration. We see signs of this restoration now, but it will not be completed until Christ returns and ends this age to usher in the next. Our assurance in Christ that God will permanently remove suffering gives us hope even in the midst of pain. In fact we can even rejoice in suffering because it increases our faith and strengthens our communion with Jesus Christ. Suffering now is part of God's plan as he leads us to the completion of his work of restoration in which our suffering will come to an end. This is God's wisdom and it is eternal good news.

CHAPTER 5

The True Gospel

Conrad Mbewe

The saying is trustworthy and deserving of full acceptance, that Christ Jesus came into the world to save sinners, of whom I am the foremost. (1 Timothy 1:15)

One of the greatest wonders of the world has been the spread of Christianity. Defying power and persecution, the Christian faith has and continues to spread across the globe, bringing together people of every race and culture. Many other movements have started in history and come to nothing. Gamaliel expected the same to happen to Christianity when he counselled the Sanhedrin (Acts 5:34-39).

But the Christian faith, once the creed of a few people in Jerusalem and Judea, is cherished and preached from Africa to Korea to South America. And this is happening despite the bitter opposition that Christians have endured from the first century to the twenty-first. Missionaries and preachers, particularly, have often paid the ultimate price for sharing what they know simply as *the good news*. Surely, one must ask, 'Why is this so? What is it that fuels this movement and makes it, against the odds, unstoppable?'

Good news is indeed the heart of it. Christians know that we have the best, most important, and most joyful news in the universe: "that Christ Jesus came into the world to save sinners" (1 Tim. 1:15). *Gospel* is an old English word that simply means good news; as does the word used in the New Testament - *evangelion*. Our message of salvation through Jesus Christ is good news, and we do not and cannot keep it to ourselves.

Furthermore, we dare not, both for our sake and the benefit of those who have not yet believed, lose sight of the true gospel. It is in Jesus Christ himself that we are reminded of what makes this news so good: his identity, interest, and intervention.

The Identity of the Saviour

The Christian message is the best news in the universe, firstly, because of the *identity* of the Saviour. Jesus Christ said: "I am the way, and the truth, and the life. No one comes to the Father except through me" (John 14:6). It is not through Mohammed, or Buddha, or the Virgin Mary, or some other religious leader, even within Christianity, that we are saved. Neither is it through an African ancestral spirit, but through Jesus Christ alone that we can be snatched from sin and hell and given grace and heaven instead. But who is this Jesus who makes such a stupendous claim?

Firstly, he is the promised *Messiah* (Christ) about whom the Old Testament prophets spoke and wrote—the hope for the people of Israel and the world. Look at what Psalms 2 and 45 say about the Messiah's unique power and authority. Meanwhile, Genesis 49:10 states that he would be born from the tribe of Judah in the nation of Israel. In Isaiah 7:14 we hear the mystery that he will be born of a virgin, while Micah 5:2 gives us the exact birthplace; Bethlehem. And in many scriptures we see that this Messiah will be a member of David's family (e.g. Isa. 11). Most amazingly, Isaiah 53 tells us that he would suffer terribly, die for our sake, and rise again from the dead. There is only one person in history who fulfilled all those prophecies, written hundreds of years prior to their fulfilment. It was Jesus Christ.

The Gospel writers in the New Testament do not want you to miss the significance of this. As Matthew wrote a number of times about Jesus' time on earth, "This took place to fulfil what was spoken by the prophet." Incredible! Jesus himself once stood up in a synagogue, read from the prophet Isaiah, and announced that the text was, in fact, about him (Luke 4:16-21).

Imagine how staggering that must have been to those who were listening. On another occasion, Jesus rebuked his disciples for failing to see all that the Old Testament had said about him, including the fact that he would suffer, die, and be raised from the dead (Luke 24:25-27; 44-47). It is this same Jesus that the apostle Paul is referring to when he says: "Christ Jesus came into the world to save sinners". He is the person that is being proclaimed to the world.

Do not miss the importance of those four words: *came into the world.* Unlike all the false messiahs and disappointing leaders who promise much and deliver little, Jesus Christ is not from this world. This Jesus Christ, the Bible teaches, is not only the ultimate man, but also God. He is the incarnate second person of the blessed Holy Trinity; the Son of God.

Every Gospel (Matthew, Mark, Luke, and John) delivers this message and the Apostle John begins his Gospel with these words:

> *In the beginning was the Word, and the Word was with God, and the Word was God. He was in the beginning with God. All things were made through him, and without him was not anything made that was made ... And the Word became flesh and dwelt among us, and we have seen his glory, glory as of the only Son from the Father, full of grace and truth. (John 1:1-3; 14)*

At each end of Jesus' earthly life, it was made abundantly clear that he is the Son of God. Before he was born, an angel told Mary that the one to be born from her womb would be the Son of God (Luke 1:35). And at the end of his life, when he breathed his last and died on the cross, the soldier who stood by and witnessed his death confessed: "Truly this was the Son of God" (Matt. 27:54). In case we missed the point, God the Father twice announced from heaven that Jesus was his Son (Matt. 3:17 and Matt. 17:5).

Why is Jesus Christ's identity such good news? However big your sin problem might be, Omnipotence has come into the world to deliver you. If Jesus was a mere human being we would despair because such a deliverer would not be powerful enough; he would have his own sins, failures, and weaknesses to overcome before he could even *attempt* to rescue us from our sins. But Christ is the holy, sinless, and all-powerful Son of God. Is anything too hard for him? (Luke 18:27) He who created this vast universe from nothing and upholds it with his all-powerful hand; can he fail to deal with the chains of sin that hold us in enslavement? No, he cannot fail. Once he hears your cry and goes into action, the strongest chains of sin give way faster than cobwebs do before an approaching flame. Praise the Lord!

The Interest of the Saviour

What makes the Christian message the best news is, secondly, the *interest* of the Saviour. As already cited, Paul wrote under the Spirit's inspiration that "Christ Jesus came into the world to save *sinners*." This is not just great news; it is shocking news.

Our consciences tell us that God is holy, so how could the Son of God come into the world seeking fellowship with *sinners*? This is what confused the Pharisees. They expected Jesus (even though they thought he was just a teacher) to shun sinners, but to their surprise he sought them out and welcomed them. "Now the tax collectors and sinners were all drawing near to hear him," Luke tells us. "And the Pharisees and the scribes grumbled, saying, 'This man receives sinners and eats with them'" (Luke 15:1-2). Yet, Jesus did not apologise about this. Rather, he answered by saying, "Those who are well have no need of a physician, but those who are sick. I have not come to call the righteous but sinners to repentance" (Luke 5:31-32).

Jesus's great interest in saving sinners is also surprising because God is the one whose law we break each time we sin. He is the offended party. When was the last time you heard of an offended person going out of his way to bless the offender? In my pre-teen years, I was often involved in childhood pranks. I recall how, as a result, the sight of a policeman would often send me into panic mode. My conscience always caused me to think that the cop was looking for me; I would quickly find a way to get out of sight. That is how our consciences ought to react when we think of God's Son coming into the world. We know that we deserve punishment from him for all the sins we have committed *against him*. Yet, amazingly, Jesus Christ came into the world, not to punish sinners, but to save them from sin (John 3:17).

Let this truth sink into your being. It was not for the righteous that Jesus came. He came for sinners. The reason why God can be interested in the welfare of sinners is because he is merciful, loving, and also *gracious*. Grace is one step higher than mercy. Grace is mercy shown by an offended party towards the person who has offended him. For example, if I found you being beaten by a mob and then rescued you from its wrath, you would call that mercy. It is human sympathy that would drive me to help you escape the clutches of that mob. However, imagine if a few days before this unfortunate event, you had come to my home and broken all my windows with a cricket bat. If then I found you being beaten up by a mob, you would expect me to join it in giving you a good-hiding. However, if instead I rescue you and even take you to a nearby hospital and pay your medical bill—that is more than mercy. That is grace.

God is gracious to sinners; even the worst of sinners. The Apostle Paul gave himself as an example of the people Jesus Christ saves: "Christ Jesus came into the world to save sinners, *of whom I am the foremost*" (1 Tim. 1:15).

Paul is insisting that he was the worst of sinners. Before his conversion, Paul insulted and said foul things against Jesus Christ, the Son of God. He made Christians suffer because of their faith in the Lord Jesus Christ. In fact, he was on his way to Damascus to get even more Christians flogged and jailed when he was converted.

That made Paul a prime example of our Saviour's interest. "But I received mercy for this reason, that in me, as the foremost, Jesus Christ might display his perfect patience as an example to those who were to believe in him for eternal life" (1 Tim. 1:16). In having mercy on the chief of sinners, God wanted to encourage other sinners not to run away from him but to apply for clemency in a similar way. If God can, in Christ, pardon big sinners like Paul, he can pardon sinners like you and me.

Perhaps that is your problem. Deep down, you know it is not about more money or a healthy body. You have sinned against God "big time" (as we say) and you are trying to avoid that reality. Perhaps you have murdered a baby in your womb and your conscience screams at you in the quietness of your soul. Maybe you have lived a sexually immoral life and you know that God is fully aware of this because he sees everything done in secret. Perhaps you have lived your life by defrauding other people and this comes back to haunt you, as you look unsatisfied at all your ill-gotten property.

"How can God forgive this?" you ask yourself. That is your biggest problem. Well, the good news of the Christian faith is that God is interested in you. He sent his Son into the world, not to condemn the world, but that the world might be saved through him (John 3:17). Believe it! He is interested in your salvation. That is why this is such good news. It is almost too good to be true. There is hope for you in spite of all your sins. Though deserving of hell, you too can spend eternity in heaven.

The Intervention of the Saviour

The Christian message is the best news in the universe, finally, because of the *intervention* of the Saviour. "Christ Jesus came into the world to *save* sinners." If a person must be saved, it is because he is in trouble and cannot save himself. One who needs saving is helpless and unable to change his circumstances. Without a rescuer, he is left to his fate.

When we think of rescue, we may picture a team of commandos sent deep into enemy territory to rescue hostages; or of a helicopter carrying lifeguards to the high seas to pull individuals from a sinking ship. Perhaps we think of a United Nations plane which goes into a famine-stricken region to deliver food and basic medical supplies to starving families. In each case, the people receiving help cannot help themselves. It is impossible. If they are not rescued, they will perish.

Jesus Christ has initiated just such an intervention. But the danger is one that not only murderers or thieves are in; we all need rescuing from our sin. Right at the beginning of history, our first parents, Adam and Eve, sinned against God by eating of the tree from which God had told them not to eat (Gen. 3). This self-centred rebellion against God had consequences that have come to each and every one of their descendants, including you and me. Since then, we are all naturally sinners.

Like Adam and Eve, we have also all sinned and "the wages of sin is death" (Rom. 6:23). Has Jesus saved you from the consequences of your sinful nature and your sins? If not, these wages are still yours to pay. That's why the Bible says, "But as for the cowardly, the faithless, the detestable, as for murderers, the sexually immoral, sorcerers, idolaters, and all liars, their portion will be in the lake that burns with fire and sulphur, which is the second death" (Rev. 21:8). All unsaved sinners will have to spend all eternity in this lake of fire.

Hell is a permanent separation from God for those never reconciled to God. We are born self-centred and enslaved to degrading morals; we are spiritually dead. Writing to those brought to life in Christ, Paul says, "And you were dead in the trespasses and sins in which you once walked, following the course of this world ... carrying out the desires of the body and the mind, and were by nature children of wrath, like the rest of mankind" (Eph. 2:1-3). It is this state of sin that makes us so desperately need a Saviour.

We *cannot* save ourselves. If it was simply good health or a fat bank account that we needed, we could have managed without a Saviour. A teacher coaching good principles of hygiene and economics has often done the trick and, through such advice, people have gone from declining health to wholesome bodies and from poverty to riches. Do you think poverty and sickness required a sacrificial rescue mission from the Son of God? We need the intervention of a Saviour because without it we will have an everlasting death.

How has Jesus Christ intervened to save us from this desperate situation? It was by his sinless life, substitutionary death on the cross, and triumph over death in resurrection. This is the pinnacle of the good news of the Christian faith. "While we were still weak, at the right time Christ died for the ungodly" (Rom. 5:6). Jesus, the Son of

God, came into this world totally sinless and he obeyed God the Father perfectly. Death had absolutely no claim on him. But then he took upon himself our liability—our guilt—and died our death on the cross as our substitute. The Bible says, "For our sake he made him to be sin who knew no sin, so that in him we might become the righteousness of God" (2 Cor. 5:21). To show that God was fully satisfied with this death on our behalf, three days later, he raised Jesus from the dead. Thus, all those who believe in Jesus, even though they die, will rise again and be with God forever. Their debt has been fully paid for in the death of Christ on the cross.

God did not even end his rescue mission there. When Jesus rose from the dead, he went to the Father in heaven and they sent the Holy Spirit to be his people's comforter and counsellor. The Holy Spirit comes into our hearts and brings us spiritual life, giving us fellowship with God and the power to deny ourselves, to love others, and to love and obey God.

Therefore, the gospel of Jesus Christ is "the power of God for salvation to everyone who believes" (Rom. 1:16). It changes people—not from the outside in as false teachers claim—but from the inside out, fitting them for eternity in God's presence. Paul marvels at this transformation at work in the Corinthian believers. "Do not be deceived: neither the sexually immoral, nor idolaters, nor adulterers, nor men who practice homosexuality, nor thieves, nor the greedy, nor drunkards, nor revilers, nor swindlers will inherit the kingdom of God." It sounds like bad news so far, yet it is the best news: "And such were some of you. But you were washed, you were sanctified, you were justified in the name of the Lord Jesus Christ and by the Spirit of our God" (1 Cor. 6:9-11).

This is the good news, which is worthy of full acceptance. It is what makes the Christian faith an unstoppable missionary movement. We have the best news in the universe: "Christ Jesus came into the world to save sinners." God himself has come down to save us. So, it does not matter how deeply enslaved you are to sin. If you recognise your desperate situation and call upon Jesus Christ to save you, he will do so. Your sins will be washed away and your heart transformed so that you start living a life that was previously impossible. Thus, you can look death in the face and not tremble because you know that its sting was removed in the death of Jesus your Saviour; all death can do is to take you to be with him in heaven. So, like a person marooned on an island who sees a helicopter hovering near him, cry to the Lord Jesus Christ and let him rescue you from death. He can do so today!

CHAPTER 6

Blessings of the True Gospel

Michael Otieno Maura

Therefore, since we have been justified by faith, we have peace with God through our Lord Jesus Christ. Through him we have also obtained access by faith into this grace in which we stand, and we rejoice in hope of the glory of God. Not only that, but we rejoice in our sufferings, knowing that suffering produces endurance, and endurance produces character, and character produces hope, and hope does not put us to shame, because God's love has been poured into our hearts through the Holy Spirit who has been given to us. (Romans 5:1-5)

There are some things that should never be far from a Christian's mind. One of them is the blessings of the gospel. What a wonderful subject. It inspires us, encourages us, humbles us, and puts the many experiences of life in perspective. Remembering the blessings that we have in God gives us the right view of him. It thrills us to live for God's glory and God's honour in this life. But in our country today, people have got the wrong concept of blessings.

For many years, I was preaching in Massai. And now that I have come to Nairobi, people are telling me that I am blessed simply because I have moved from a rural area to the big city. Many Christians have this wrong concept of blessing that focuses their hearts and minds on worldly benefits and passing pleasures. God knows our hearts and has warned us of, and corrected, this error in Scripture.

Paul wrote to Christians living in one of the greatest and most powerful cities of the ancient world – Rome. All around them they would have seen wealth, power, and status flaunted and glorified. But Paul was not interested in any of this. His focus was on the gospel. In chapter 1, he describes the gospel as "the power of God for salvation to everyone who believes" (Rom. 1:16). And not only that, "in it the righteousness of God is revealed ... as it is written, "The righteous shall live by faith" (Rom. 1:17).

But in order to recognise the power and grace of the gospel, we have to see our real situation. So in verse 18, Paul proclaims that "the wrath of God is revealed from heaven against all ungodliness and unrighteousness of men." This is relevant for us all because, in chapter 2, Paul makes it clear that *the whole world* is guilty before God.

The bad news prepares us for the good news. In chapter 3 from verse 21, we can see the beauty of justification by faith; that we are not made right with God through anything that we do. But we are made right with God only through faith in the Lord Jesus Christ.

This is not a new concept. In chapter 4 there are examples of two people who were justified, made right with God, by faith in him. Both Abraham and David were justified through faith alone. This has always been the way God works.

When Paul began chapter 5 with the word *therefore*, he did not want us to miss his point. After he had described the faith of Abraham, Paul continued *"therefore*, since we have been justified by faith, we have peace with God through our Lord Jesus Christ." This is the way—Paul wanted us to see—that God *saves*. Justification by faith is biblical.

So let me clarify and define what justification by faith means. Justification by faith is an act of God's free grace. God, on his own initiative, forgives and pardons all our sins and declares us righteous in his sight because of the righteousness of Christ imputed to us. And we receive this gift only by faith in the finished work of the Lord Jesus Christ alone. That is justification by faith.

It is hard for people to accept that they are not in charge. Every person wants to believe that he is the hero of his own story. But God gives justification freely; we cannot earn it. Remember that Luther re-discovered, reading Romans 1:17, that the righteous live by faith. This discovery transformed his life. The Holy Spirit illuminated his mind and all of a sudden the man who had been sweating and agonising to earn his salvation realised that man is justified by faith.

Are we preaching this? Are we liberated by the message of justification by faith or do we still think that we are justified through what we do? Are we embracing justification by faith with all our hearts and strength? We need people who will go out there and let Africa know that God justifies by faith.

Blessing Number One: Peace with God

Once Paul had explained justification by faith, he told the Romans about the benefits and blessings which it brings. This chapter is about the blessings of the gospel of justification by faith. We can see the first blessing in that first verse of chapter five: "Therefore, since we have been justified by faith, we have *peace with God* through our Lord Jesus Christ."

Remember what we saw in Romans 1:18: the whole world is guilty. This is a problem that only God can solve. "But God shows his love for us in that while we were still sinners, Christ died for us" (Rom. 5:8). This is the power and purpose of Christ's death: "while we were enemies we were reconciled to God" (Rom. 5:10). Paul was not talking mainly about inward peace; an experience or a feeling. This is about a broken relationship with God that he has restored.

A sinner is God's enemy. Without faith in Jesus Christ, we are still at war with God. Why? God is holy and righteous, but we have rejected his righteousness. God is exalted above everything else and he dwells in holiness, yet we have chosen to fight against his holiness with our self-centred sin. Our self-centredness gets us nowhere because God requires nothing less than righteousness. And none of us is righteous (Rom. 3:9-18, 23).

Therefore, we need this justification so that we may have peace with God. We are all sinful because of our perverted human nature. Adam's sin was imputed to us; we are the heirs of Adam who disobeyed God and brought sin into the human race. And so, from birth, we are at war with God. He is holy and requires holiness, but we fall short of that holiness.

Any honest assessment will conclude that our nature is corrupt. Our emotions, our understanding, our words, and our actions all separate us from God. We cannot have a good relationship with God by our own efforts. We are not only sinful in Adam, but we ourselves also sin and desire sin. And God condemns sinners because he is just.

So can you understand that peace with God is an amazing blessing? It should thrill us that a sinner—condemned, wretched, deserving justice—can now have peace with God. If you are justified by faith, you are reconciled; you are at a place of peace with your maker. This is what we should be saying every Sunday: man can have peace with God. Christians are no longer at war with God. We are now on God's side.

What are the implications and consequences of this peace with God? Firstly, we do not need to question our relationship with our God. The punishment which should have fallen on us, fell on our substitute on the cross of Calvary. And the righteousness of the Lord Jesus Christ has been imputed to us. When God looks at us, he no longer sees us; he sees the righteousness of his Son and we are right in his sight.

I have a daughter who is in primary school. When a bill comes for fees, I go to the school and I give the headmaster money. So when someone asks the class how many people have paid, she will raise her hand, even though she did not give the money. The money is mine, but she is considered to have paid. That is what God has done for us in Christ. So when the devil reminds us of our sin and makes us doubt our relationship with God, we have an answer. God's righteousness has been credited to us through the Lord Jesus Christ. We have peace with God through Jesus.

And so the peace that Jesus Christ has bought between us and God also brings peace into our hearts. Our consciences no longer keep us from God. When we are justified and the righteousness of Christ is imputed to us, our consciences no longer accuse us. The justice of God has been met in the Lord Jesus Christ's death for us. Satan can accuse us, but he cannot condemn us because we have been justified by God himself.

Are we teaching this? I remember a young man who came to me some years back and told me, "Pastor, I backslid last night" and I said: "Why?" He said to me: "I dreamt that I was drunk, so my salvation is gone." This is a result of the fact that we are not grounding people in the truth that salvation *does not depend on us*. Justification does not depend on what we do; it depends on what the Lord Jesus Christ has done and on his righteousness. There are many people who are worried about their salvation and they need us to go and tell them that if you are justified by faith in Christ Jesus, you have everlasting peace with God. "There is now *no condemnation* for those who are in Christ Jesus" (Rom. 8:1).

The Only Way to Peace with God

So that is blessing number one: "Therefore, since we have been justified by faith, we have *peace with God* through our Lord Jesus Christ" (Rom 5:1). Before moving on to the next blessing, I want to emphasise that word *through*.

Some people think and act as though peace with God can be won in other ways. But Paul made it clear that peace with God is only *through the Lord Jesus Christ*. He is the only mediator between man and God. There is no other way to have this great blessing of peace with God. It must be through Jesus Christ.

We had a very small post office where I lived. I was in a village called Ugunja. If you wrote to us, you had to write on the letter: PO Box 13, Ugunja, *via* Siaya. In order to get to us, that letter had to go via Siaya. And this peace with God is via Jesus Christ. There is no other route. It is the Lord Jesus Christ who has lived a perfect life. And his perfect life fulfilled the law on our behalf. Only the Lord Jesus Christ has lived a perfect life without sin.

Jesus Christ is the one who atoned for our sin by his precious blood. He is the only one who has satisfied God's moral law. He is the only man who has met God's standard of perfection. And therefore peace with God is through Jesus Christ. Are we telling people this every Sunday? Does our daily life show that we believe that peace with God is through the Lord Jesus Christ?

You can receive an anointing on your head or on your feet or you can swim in the pool. That cannot bring peace with God; it will not. That is the work of paganism and it must be thrown out. We must go and tell people: you can have peace with God through Jesus Christ and through Jesus Christ alone.

One of my favourite passages that highlights the sufficiency of Christ for everything is 1 Corinthians 1:30-31: "And because of him [God] you are in Christ Jesus, who became to us wisdom from God, righteousness and sanctification and redemption, so that, as it is written, 'Let the one who boasts, boast in the Lord.'"

Like the rich young man in the gospels, some people go away sad when we preach of the eternal blessings of the gospel. But peace with God does not come through material possessions. Think of the men who are preaching the gospel in the rural corners of this land. Those pastors who are labouring with no shoes and no bicycles are richly blessed. They have peace with God and they are proclaiming this peace with God through Jesus Christ. That is what we must stand for.

Blessing Number Two: Access to God

We see the next blessing in verse two of Romans 5: "Through him we have also obtained *access by faith* into this grace in which we stand." Now, because we have been justified and have peace with God, we also have *access to God*. We have obtained access, which we do not deserve, to the throne of grace before which we now stand.

We used to be rebels barred from God's presence. Let me give you an example. During the Kenyan elections of 1992, in the time of President Moi, many people defected from their parties to join KANU (Moi's party). These defectors came from rural areas to the State House and they were brought into the President's chamber. They enjoyed food there and met with the President. And the President even started going on the campaign trail with them. They used to be opposed to the President, but now they had access, overflowing access, to the State House.

In a similar way, each of us was a rebel against God. But the Lord Jesus Christ, since we have been justified by faith, has led us to God himself. And now we have access. We have been ushered into the presence of God. His justification brings us security and confidence before our God.

The presence of God has always been important to God's people. Remember that the Temple was a sign of God's presence with his people. But even the Temple was divided into three: the holy of holies, the holy place, and the outer court. In the holy of holies was the mercy seat; only the high priest could enter that place and he did so only once a year to make a sacrifice for the people's sins. But the sacrifice for us has been made once and for all. And so, now we are brought by the Lord Jesus into the very presence of the Most High God. We have access to God.

The writer of the book of Hebrews summarised it well in Hebrews 4:14-16:

> *Since then we have a great high priest who has passed through the heavens, Jesus, the Son of God, let us hold fast our confession. For we do not have a high priest who is unable to sympathize with our weaknesses, but one who in every respect has been tempted as we are, yet without sin. Let us then with confidence draw near to the throne of grace, that we may receive mercy and find grace to help in time of need.*

What we have in Jesus Christ is better than what the Old Testament saints had. In the Lord Jesus Christ, you have a high priest who gives you access to God. Therefore, you can now go to the throne of grace with boldness. We have gained access through Jesus Christ and so we come with confidence. This is a great blessing.

But we must not get the wrong idea about the confidence that we can and should have in Jesus. God is a consuming fire. We dare not mess around with God. We see in the Bible the fate of those who dishonour and disregard God. He is holy and set apart and he demands our reverence. When we go to him, we do not go to argue or demand.

This confidence is our knowledge that the access Christ has won for us, and we have received by faith, is not in doubt. God has done it and it is sure. Imagine you have been invited to a wedding. And if they asked you at the entrance why you should be allowed in, you would produce your invitation. You are invited; you do not need to worry. The Lord Jesus Christ has invited us and has given us his righteousness. We do not go in confidence because of our own achievements. But we go in confidence because he has washed us with his blood and his righteousness has been given to us. It is confidence based on what the Lord Jesus Christ has done on our behalf.

Despite the fact that we have access to God, some churches and preachers try to put a barrier between Christians and God. We do not need a priest to give us access to God. But it is not only Catholic priests who set themselves up as gatekeepers to the throne of grace. We have many churches that have fallen to the temptation of the personality cult. The pastor is the only one who can pray for you. He is the only one who can bless you. If he goes on safari in Tanzania, you need to ask him to say a prayer for you over the phone. Christians need to be taught that they have access to God through Christ.

In most of our cultures, we are used to having people represent us; people who stand in between us and God. But this is not fruit of the gospel. Every believer in the Lord Jesus Christ has obtained access to God. And this is not by our work, by the money we give, by our strength, by our abilities, or by our background. It is simply because

God has declared us righteous on the merit of his son that we have this great blessing of access to God.

Blessing Number Three: Joy from the Hope of God's Glory

But there are more blessings to come. Peace with God and access to God in Christ Jesus give us *joy* because of the hope they give us. Look at Romans 5:2 again: "Through him we have also obtained access by faith into this grace in which we stand, and we *rejoice in hope of the glory of God.*"

This word *rejoice* is also translated as *boast* and if we combine those two words, we get a good idea of Paul's meaning. What he is talking about is an enthusiastic confidence in something beautiful.[i] When we know that something precious—a person, a gift, a treasure—is reliably ours, the experience of that *is* joy. In Jesus we are sure of our claim on the very best thing. We rejoice in the hope of the glory of God. Paul told the Romans, look: Abraham was justified by faith. David was justified by faith. And the atoning work of the Lord Jesus Christ on Calvary has given us peace with God. It has given us access. And because of this we can now rejoice in the hope of sharing the glory of God.

But just as we have to be careful to define *blessing*, the words *joy* and *rejoice* are also misused today. This joy we are talking about does not come as a result of what we obtain on the outside. It is a joy that comes as a result of us being justified by faith in Christ Jesus. Joy is not de-

---

i   Darrell Bock, *The Bible Knowledge Word Study: Acts-Ephesians* (Colorado Springs: Cook, 2006), 152.

fined by noise or laughter. I have seen people laughing the whole night, claiming that to be the joy of the Lord. That is not the joy of the Lord. The joy Paul told us about is a delight in the certainty of eternal blessing. We are sure that we are going to share the glory of God.

This is not a vague hope, like hoping to get a good job or a nice house in the future. This is being sure that one day we shall see the glory of God who has justified us. Without any shadow of a doubt we know that he has saved us; he has rescued us, and we are going to share his glory. In Colossians 1:27 it says: "Christ in you, the hope of glory." If you have the Lord Jesus Christ in you, then you can have the hope of glory.

And we do not hope for something which is yet to exist. God is not fooling us. His glory has been there for all time and it sustains the world. One day it will cover the earth and we will share in it. If you have watched a play in a theatre, you know that there is a curtain on the stage. Before the drama begins, the curtain is closed. But the players are already there and the audience is waiting for the curtain to be removed. When the curtain is removed, you see everything that was already there. The glory of God is there and one day those who are justified by faith will not only see it but they will also share in it.

Have you lost interest in the glory of God? The world tries to distract us with the desire of sin and some want to exchange the glory of God for what they can have here and now. But we have something more precious than gold, silver, or anything else this world has to offer. We have the hope of the glory of God. You cannot find this blessing outside of the gospel of Jesus Christ.

Our Lord Jesus knows that sharing in the glory of God is an incomparable blessing. He earnestly desires it for us, praying for it: "Father, I desire that they also, whom you have given me, may be with me where I am, to see my glory that you have given me because you loved me before the foundation of the world" (John 17:24). Christians have the sure hope of sharing in the glory of God. And this hope gives them joy.

Blessing Number Four: Joy in Suffering

The world promises us things that fade away and crumble into dust. The blessings we have in the gospel last forever. And so another blessing we have is that, even in our suffering, we can rejoice. "Not only that, but *we rejoice in our sufferings*, knowing that suffering produces endurance" (Rom. 5:3). We can take delight in our sufferings. What a strange blessing.

If you preach this in some churches, people become gloomy. There used to be a church in Nairobi that had a big banner: "Stop suffering - by joining the Universal Church of Christ." The Bible does not promise this, but it does say we can rejoice in our sufferings. Should we remove this verse from the Bible? No. We should bow our heads and thank God. Those who have been justified, even though facing persecution, can and do rejoice. How can this be?

Firstly, suffering is a vital means of our sanctification. We can rejoice in suffering because tribulation produces perseverance. (There is also bad suffering. If I am punished for stealing; that is not for the glory of God and it is not Christian suffering.) When we face trouble because we trust in the Lord Jesus Christ, God uses that to strengthen our faith. Have you been ridiculed for your faith? When we hold on to Christ through that, God uses it to strengthen our grip on him. And the next time it happens, we hold yet more firmly to him. Suffering produces perseverance in faith.

And perseverance, Paul tells us, produces character. A faithful Christian is a person who has gone through trouble and has been trained and moulded by it. Remember David's experience and how it shaped his character. When Saul asked him if he would be able to fight against Goliath, he had a ready answer. He looked after his father's sheep and when a lion or a bear had attacked the sheep, he had killed that attacker. He had experienced how God helped him when he was threatened and it built his character. So he could say: "The LORD who delivered me from the paw of the lion and the paw of the bear will deliver me from the hand of this Philistine" (1 Sam. 17:37). Suffering produces character.

We also rejoice in suffering because it reveals the power of God. One of my teachers, Martin Bussey, used to give us an example of a missionary who went to preach in a certain place and there was no fruit for a long time. Then one of his children became sick and eventually died. This missionary, as a child of God, did not suffer or grieve as the world does (1 Thess. 4:13). And the people took note. They saw the way he handled the sickness and death of his child and they wondered why he was different. And the next day people started coming. The way a Christian handles suffering reveals the power of God. The world is able to see the power of God and the grace of God in our lives. And it draws people to our Saviour.

Suffering also prepares us for future usefulness. Can you imagine a preacher who is not sympathetic? Sometimes preachers need to experience suffering even for the benefit of others. When we experience suffering, we are more able to sympathise with, and minister to, those who suffer.

Also, the ministry of a suffering Christian carries a special power to feed our souls. I must mention the late John Nkarithia in Maithene-Meru. He went through a lot of suffering and sickness and he glorified God in it. If you went to see him, you thought you would encourage him. But you were the one who would leave the place encouraged. In fact, before he died he even prayed for me to go and preach the gospel. We glorify God in our suffering when we use it to teach others.

Please be ready to prepare people for death. Do not just pray for people to be healed. Pray and prepare them for glory. I read Romans 8:18-39 to John Nkarithia: "I consider that our present sufferings are not worth comparing with the glory that is to be revealed to us" (Rom. 8:18). The time has come for us to know, as this brother did, that we are able to rejoice in our sufferings.

And the hope that sustains us and sanctifies us in our suffering does not disappoint. The love of God has been poured into our hearts. We have a hope which is certain. In fact, Paul, writing to Timothy, said, "Christ Jesus our hope" (1 Tim. 1:1). Jesus is our hope. The hope which is in the Lord Jesus Christ does not disappoint.

Conclusion

You see the Trinity in the blessings of the gospel. God the Father sent God the Son to take the punishment we deserve so that we can have peace with God and access to him. And he has poured love and joy and hope into our hearts by the Holy Spirit who he has given to us. This joy of the hope of the glory of God sustains us even through suffering, which only brings us closer to God and strengthens our faith.

These are some of the blessings which we have through the gospel of justification by faith in Jesus. Do we teach these blessings? Are we talking about these blessings? Do we know these blessings? Are we rejoicing in these blessings? Thanks to the great love of God, which has been poured in our hearts, we are blessed with peace, security, hope, and joy that will last forever.

Twelve Appeals to Prosperity Preachers

John Piper

Don't Make Heaven Harder

Jesus said, "How difficult it will be for those who have wealth to enter the kingdom of God!" His disciples were astonished, as many in the "prosperity" movement should be. So Jesus went on to raise their astonishment even higher by saying, "It is easier for a camel to go through the eye of a needle than for a rich person to enter the kingdom of God." They responded in disbelief: "Then who can be saved?" Jesus says, "With man it is impossible, but not with God. For all things are possible with God" (Mark 10:23-27).

This means that their astonishment was warranted. A camel can't go through the eye of a needle. This is not a metaphor for something requiring great effort or humble sacrifice. It can't be done. We know that because Jesus said, *Impossible!* That was his word, not ours. "With man it is impossible." The point is that the heart-change required is something man can't do for himself. God must do it - "...but [it is] not [impossible] with God."

We can't make ourselves stop treasuring money above Christ. But God can. That is good news. And that should be part of the message that prosperity preachers herald before they entice people to become more camel-like. Why would a preacher want to preach a gospel that encourages the desire to be rich and thus confirms people in their natural unfitness for the kingdom of God?

Save People from Suicide

The apostle Paul warned against the *desire* to be rich. And by implication, he warned against preachers who stir up the desire to be rich instead of helping people get rid of it. He warned,

> *Those who desire to be rich fall into temptation, into a snare, into many senseless and harmful desires that plunge people into ruin and destruction. For the love of money is a root of all kinds of evils. It is through this craving that some have wandered away from the faith and pierced themselves with many pangs. (1 Tim. 6:9-10)*

These are very serious words, but they don't seem to find an echo in the preaching of the prosperity gospel. It is not wrong for the poor to want measures of prosperity so that they have what they need and can be generous and can devote time and energy to Christ-exalting tasks other than scraping to get by. It is not wrong to seek Christ for help in this quest. He cares about our needs (Matt. 6:33).

But we all—poor and rich—are constantly in danger of setting our affections (1 John 2:15-16) and our hope (1 Tim. 6:17) on riches rather than Christ. This "desire to be rich" is so strong and so suicidal that Paul uses the strongest language to warn us. My appeal is that prosperity preachers would do the same.

Warn Against Weak Investments

Jesus warns against the effort to lay up treasures on earth; that is, he tells us to be *givers*, not *keepers*. "Do not lay up for yourselves treasures on earth, where moth and rust destroy and where thieves break in and steal, but lay up for yourselves treasures in heaven, where neither moth nor rust destroys and where thieves do not break in and steal" (Matt. 6:19-20).

Yes, we all keep something. Jesus assumes that. He does not expect, except in extreme cases, that our giving will mean we will no longer be able to give. There may be a time when we will give our life for someone and thus no longer be able to give any more. But ordinarily Jesus expects us to live in a way that there is an ongoing pattern of work and earning and simple living and continual giving.

But given the built-in tendency toward greed in all of us, Jesus feels the need to warn against "laying up treasures on earth." It looks like gain, but it leads only to loss ("moth and rust destroy and thieves break in and steal"). My appeal is that Jesus' warning find a strong echo in the mouths of prosperity preachers.

Grow Lavish Givers

Getting rich is not what work is for. Paul said we should not steal. The alternative was hard work with our own hands. But the main purpose was not merely to hoard or even to *have*. The purpose was "to have *in order to give*."

"Let the thief no longer steal, but rather let him labour, doing honest work with his own hands, *so that he may have something to share* with anyone in need" (Eph. 4:28). This is not a justification for being rich in order to give more. It is a call to make more and keep less so you can give more. There is no reason why a person who prospers more and more in his business should increase the lavishness of his lifestyle indefinitely. Paul would say, cap your expenditures and give the rest away.

I can't determine your "cap." But in all the texts we are looking at in this chapter, there is an impulse toward simplicity and lavish generosity, not lavish possessions. When Jesus said, "Sell your possessions, and give to the needy" (Luke 12:33), he seemed to imply not that the disciples were wealthy and could give from their overflow. It seems they had so few liquid assets that they had to sell something in order to have something to give.

Why would preachers want to encourage people to think that they should possess wealth in order to be a lavish giver? Why not encourage them to keep their lives more simple and be an even more lavish giver? Would that not add to their generosity a strong testimony that Christ, and not possessions, is their treasure?

Foster Faith in God

The reason the writer to the Hebrews tells us to be content with what we have is that the opposite implies less faith in the promises of God. He says, "Keep your life free from love of money, and be content with what you have, for he has said, 'I will never leave you nor forsake you.' So we can confidently say, 'The Lord is my helper; I will not fear; what can man do to me?'" (Heb. 13:5-6).

On the one hand, we may trust in the Lord to be our helper. He will provide and protect. And in that sense there is a measure of prosperity he will give us. "Your heavenly Father knows that you need them all" (Matt. 6:32). But, on the other hand, when it says, "Keep your life free from love of money, and be content with what you have" *because* God promises never to leave us, it must mean that we can easily move from trusting God for our *needs* to using God for our wants.

The line between "God help me," and "God make me rich," is real, and the writer to the Hebrews doesn't want us to cross it. Preachers should help their people to remember and recognize this line rather than speaking as though it weren't there.

Eliminate Choking Hazards

Jesus warns that the word of God, the gospel, which is meant to give us life, can be choked to death by riches. He says it is like a seed that grows up among thorns: "They are those who hear, but as they go on their way they are choked by the ... riches ... of life, and their fruit does not mature" (Luke 8:14).

Prosperity preachers should warn their hearers that there is a kind of financial prosperity that can choke them to death. Why would we want to encourage people to pursue the very thing that Jesus warns can make them fruitless?

Preserve the Salt and Light

What is it about Christians that makes them the salt of the earth and the light of the world? It is not wealth. The desire for wealth and the pursuit of wealth tastes and looks just like the world. Desiring to be rich makes us *like* the world, not different. At the very point where we should taste different, we have the same bland covetousness that the world has. In that case, we don't offer the world anything different from what it already believes in.

The great tragedy of prosperity preaching is that a person does not have to be spiritually awakened in order to embrace it; one needs only to be greedy. Getting rich in the name of Jesus is not the salt of the earth or the light of the world. In this, the world simply sees a reflection of itself. And if they are "converted" to this, they have not been truly converted, but only put a new name on an old life.

The context of Jesus' saying shows us what the salt and light are. They are the joyful willingness to suffer for Christ. Here is what Jesus said,

> *Blessed are you when others revile you and persecute you and utter all kinds of evil against you falsely on my account. Rejoice and be glad, for your reward is great in heaven, for so they persecuted the prophets who were before you. You are the salt of the earth ... You are the light of the world. (Matt. 5:11-14)*

What will make the world *taste* the salt and *see* the light of Christ in us is not that we love wealth the same way they do. Rather, it will be the willingness and the ability of Christians to love others through suffering, all the while rejoicing because their reward is in heaven with Jesus. "*Rejoice* and be glad [in hardship] ... You are the salt of the earth." The saltiness is the taste of joy in hardship. This is *unusual* life that the world can taste as different.

Such life is inexplicable on human terms. It is supernatural. But to attract people with promises of prosperity is simply natural. It is not the message of Jesus. It is not what he died to achieve.

Don't Conceal the Cost

Missing from most prosperity preaching is the fact that the New Testament emphasizes the necessity of suffering far more than it does the notion of material prosperity.

Jesus said, "Remember the word that I said to you: 'A servant is not greater than his master.' If they persecuted me, they will also persecute you. If they kept my word, they will also keep yours" (John 15:20). Or again he said, "If they have called the head of the house Beelzebul, how much more *will they malign* the members of his household" (Matt. 10:25).

Paul reminded the new believers on his missionary journeys, "through many tribulations we must enter the kingdom of God" (Acts 14:22). And he told the believers in Rome that their sufferings were a necessary part of the path to eternal inheritance.

The Spirit himself bears witness with our spirit that we are children of God, and if children, then heirs—heirs of God and fellow heirs with Christ, provided we suffer with him in order that we may also be glorified with him. For I consider that the sufferings of this present time are not worth com-

*paring with the glory that is to be revealed to us.
(Rom. 8:16-18)*

Peter too said that suffering is the normal pathway to
God's eternal blessing.

*Beloved, do not be surprised at the fiery trial when
it comes upon you to test you, as though something
strange were happening to you. But rejoice insofar as you share Christ's sufferings, that you may
also rejoice and be glad when his glory is revealed.
If you are insulted for the name of Christ, you are
blessed, because the Spirit of glory and of God
rests upon you. (1 Pet. 4:12-14)*

Suffering is the normal cost of godliness. "Indeed,
all who desire to live a godly life in Christ Jesus will be
persecuted" (2 Tim. 3:12). I am aware that these words
on suffering move back and forth between a more general
suffering as part of the fall (Rom. 8:18-25) and specific
suffering owing to human hostilities. But when it comes
to God's purposes in our suffering there is no substantial
difference.

Prosperity preachers should include in their messages
significant teaching about what Jesus and the apostles
said about the necessity of suffering. It must come, Paul
said (Acts 14:22), and we do young disciples a disservice
not to tell them that early. Jesus even said it before conversion so that prospective believers would count the
cost: "So therefore, any one of you who does not renounce
all that he has cannot be my disciple" (Luke 14:33).

Uphold the Value of Suffering

The New Testament not only makes clear that suffering is necessary for followers of Christ, it is also at pains to explain why that it is the case and what God's purposes in it are. These purposes are crucial for believers to know. God has revealed them to help us understand why we suffer and to bring us through like gold through fire.

In *Let the Nations Be Glad*, in the chapter on suffering, I unfold these purposes. Here I will only name them and say to the prosperity preachers: Include the great biblical teachings in your messages. New believers need to know why God ordains for them to suffer.

1. Suffering deepens faith and holiness.
2. Suffering makes your cup increase.
3. Suffering is the price of making others bold.
4. Suffering fills up what is lacking in Christ's afflictions.
5. Suffering enforces the missionary command to go.
6. The supremacy of Christ is manifest in suffering.

Teach Them to Go

A fundamental change happened with the coming of Christ into the world. Until that time, God had focused his redemptive work on Israel with occasional works among the nations. Paul said, "In past generations [God] allowed all the nations to walk in their own ways" (Acts 14:16). He called them "times of ignorance." "The times of ignorance God overlooked, but now he commands all people everywhere to repent" (Acts 17:30). Now the focus has shifted from Israel to the nations. Jesus said, "The kingdom of God will be taken away from you [Israel] and given to a people producing its fruits [followers of the Messiah]"

(Matt. 21:43). A hardening has come upon Israel until the full number of the nations comes in (Rom. 11:25).

One of the main differences between these two eras is that in the Old Testament, God glorified himself largely by blessing Israel so that the nations could see and know that the Lord is God. "May [the Lord] maintain the cause of ... his people Israel, as each day requires, *that all the peoples of the earth may know that the Lord is God;* there is no other" (1 Kings 8:59-60). Israel was not yet sent on a "Great Commission" to gather the nations; rather, she was glorified so that the nations would see her greatness and come to her.

So when Solomon built the temple of the Lord it was spectacularly lavish with overlaid gold.

The inner sanctuary was twenty cubits long, twenty cubits wide, and twenty cubits high, and he overlaid it with pure gold. He also overlaid an altar of cedar. And Solomon overlaid the inside of the house with pure gold, and he drew chains of gold across, in front of the inner sanctuary, and overlaid it with gold. And he overlaid the whole house with gold, until all the house was finished. Also the whole altar that belonged to the inner sanctuary he overlaid with gold. (1 Kings 6:20–22)

And when he furnished it, the gold was again just as abundant.

So Solomon made all the vessels that were in the house of the Lord: the golden altar, the golden ta-ble for the bread of the Presence, the lampstands of pure gold, five on the south side and five on the

north, before the inner sanctuary; the flowers, the
lamps, and the tongs, of gold; the cups, snuffers,
basins, dishes for incense, and fire pans, of pure
gold; and the sockets of gold, for the doors of the
innermost part of the house. (1 Kings 7:48-50)

It took Solomon seven years to build the house of the
Lord. Then he took thirteen years to build his own house
(1 Kings 6:38-7:1). It too was lavish with gold and costly
stones (1 Kings 7, 10).

Then, when all was built, the point of this opulence is
seen in 1 Kings 10 as the queen of Sheba, representing
the Gentile nations, comes to see the glory of the house
of God and of Solomon. When she saw it, "there was no
more breath in her" (1 Kings 10:5). She said, "Blessed be
the Lord your God, who has delighted in you and set you
on the throne of Israel! Because the Lord loved Israel forever, he has made you king" (1 Kings 10:9).

In other words, the pattern in the Old Testament is
a come-see religion. There is a geographic center of the
people of God. There is a physical temple, an earthly king,
a political regime, an ethnic identity, an army to fight
God's earthly battles, and a band of priests to make animal sacrifices for sins.

With the coming of Christ all of this changed. There
is no geographic center for Christianity (John 4:20-24);
Jesus has replaced the temple, the priests, and the sacrifices (John 2:19; Heb. 9:25-26); there is no Christian
political regime because Christ's kingdom is not of this
world (John 18:36); and we do not fight earthly battles
with chariots and horses or bombs and bullets, but spiritual ones with the word and the Spirit (Eph. 6:12-18; 2
Cor. 10:3-5).

All of this supports the great change in mission. The New Testament does not present a come-see religion, but a go-tell religion. "And Jesus came and said to them, 'All authority in heaven and on earth has been given to me. Go therefore and make disciples of all nations, baptizing them in the name of the Father and of the Son and of the Holy Spirit, teaching them to observe all that I have commanded you. And behold, I am with you always, to the end of the age'" (Matt. 28:18-20).

The implications of this are huge for the way we live and the way we think about money and lifestyle. One of the main implications is that we are "sojourners and exiles" (1 Pet. 2:11) on the earth. We do not use this world as though it were our primary home. "Our citizenship is in heaven, and from it we await a Saviour, the Lord Jesus Christ" (Phil. 3:20).

This leads to a wartime lifestyle. That means we don't amass wealth to show the world how rich our God can make us. We work hard and seek a wartime austerity for the cause of spreading the gospel to the ends of the earth. We maximize giving to the war effort, not comforts at home. We raise our children with a view to helping them embrace the suffering that it will cost to finish the mission.

So if a prosperity preacher asks me about all the promises of wealth for faithful people in the Old Testament, my response is: Read your New Testament carefully and see if you see the same emphasis. You won't find it. And the reason is that things have dramatically changed.

"We brought nothing into the world, and we cannot take anything out of the world. But if we have food and clothing, with these we will be content" (1 Tim. 6:7-8). Why? Because the call to Christ is a call to "share in suffering as a good soldier of Christ Jesus" (2 Tim. 2:3). The emphasis of the New Testament is not riches to lure us in to sin, but sacrifice to carry us out.

One providential confirmation that God intended this distinction between a come-see orientation in the Old Testament and a go-tell orientation in the New Testament is the difference between the language of the Old Testament and the language of the New. Hebrew, the language of the Old Testament, was shared by no other peoples of the ancient world. It was unique to Israel. This is an astonishing contrast with Greek, the language of the New Testament, which was the trade language of the Roman world. So the very languages of the Old and New Testaments signal the difference in mission. Hebrew was not well-suited for missions to the ancient world. Greek was ideally suited for missions to the Roman world.

Separate from the Peddlers

The apostle Paul set us an example by how vigilant he was not to give the impression that he was in the ministry for money. He said that ministers of the word have a right to make a living from the ministry. But then, to show us the danger in that, he refuses to fully use that right.

It is written in the Law of Moses, "You shall not muzzle an ox when it treads out the grain." ... It was written for our sake, because the ploughman should plough in hope and the thresher thresh in hope of sharing in the crop. If we have sown spiritual things among you, is it too much if we reap material things from you? If others share this rightful claim on you, do not we even more? Nevertheless, we have not made use of this right, but

we endure anything rather than put an obstacle in
the way of the gospel of Christ. (1 Cor. 9:9-12)

In other words, he renounced a legitimate right in order not to give anyone the impression that money was the motivation of his ministry. He did not want the money of his converts: "We never came with words of flattery, as you know, nor with a pretext for greed—God is witness" (1 Thess. 2:5).

He preferred to work with his hands rather than give the impression that he was peddling the gospel:

I coveted no one's silver or gold or apparel. You
yourselves know that these hands ministered to
my necessities and to those who were with me. In
all things I have shown you that by working hard
in this way we must help the weak and remember
the words of the Lord Jesus, how he himself said,
'It is more blessed to give than to receive.' (Acts
20:33-35)

He knew that there were peddlers of God's word who thought "godliness is a means of gain" (1 Tim. 6:5-6). But he refused to do anything that would put him in that category: "We are not, like so many, *peddlers of God's word,* but as men of sincerity, as commissioned by God, in the sight of God we speak in Christ" (2 Cor. 2:17).

Too many prosperity preachers not only give the impression that they "peddle God's word" and make "godliness a means of gain" but actually develop a bogus theology to justify their extravagant displays of wealth. Paul did just the opposite.

Commend Christ as Gain

My biggest concern about the effects of the prosperity movement is that it diminishes Christ by making him less central and less satisfying than his gifts. Christ is not magnified most by being the giver of wealth. He is magnified most by satisfying the soul of those who sacrifice to love others in the ministry of the gospel.

When we commend Christ as the one who makes us rich, we glorify riches, and Christ becomes a means to the end of what we really want—namely, health, wealth, and prosperity. But when we commend Christ as the one who satisfies our soul forever—even when there is no health, wealth, and prosperity—then Christ is magnified as more precious than all those gifts.

We see this in Philippians 1:20-21. Paul says, "It is my eager expectation and hope that ... Christ will be honoured in my body, whether by life or by death. For to me to live is Christ, and to die is gain." Honoring Christ happens when we treasure him so much that dying is *gain*. Because dying means "to depart and be with Christ" (Phil. 1:23).

This is the missing note in prosperity preaching. The New Testament aims at the glory of Christ, not the glory of his gifts. To make that clear, it puts the entire Christian life under the banner of joyful self-denial. "If anyone would come after me, let him *deny himself* and take up his cross and follow me." (Mark 8:34). "I have been crucified with Christ" (Gal. 2:20).

But even though self-denial is a hard road that leads to life (Matt. 7:14), it is the most joyful of all roads. "The kingdom of heaven is like treasure hidden in a field, which a man found and covered up. Then *in his joy* he goes and sells all that he has and buys that field" (Matt. 13:44). Jesus says that finding Christ as our treasure makes all other possessions *joyfully* dispensable. "*In his joy* he goes and sells all that he has and buys that field."

I do not want prosperity preachers to stop calling people to maximum joy. On the contrary, I appeal to them to stop encouraging people to seek their joy in material things. The joy Christ offers is so great and so durable that it enables us to lose prosperity and still rejoice. "You joyfully accepted the plundering of your property, *since you knew that you yourselves had a better possession and an abiding one*" (Heb. 10:34). The grace to be joyful in the loss of prosperity—that is the miracle prosperity preachers should seek. That would be the salt of the earth and the light of the world. That would magnify Christ as supremely valuable.

Money

Wayne Grudem

Money is fundamentally good and provides many opportunities for glorifying God, but also many temptations to sin.

People sometimes say that "money is the root of all evil," but the Bible does not say that. Paul says in 1 Timothy 6:10, the love of money is a root of all kinds of evils, but that speaks of the love of money, not money itself.

In fact, money is fundamentally good because it is a human invention that sets us apart from the animal kingdom and enables us to subdue the earth by producing from the earth goods and services that bring benefit to others. Money enables all of mankind to be productive and enjoy the fruits of that productivity thousands of times more extensively than we could if no human being had money, and we just had to barter with each other.

Without money, I would have only one thing to trade with, and that is copies of my books. I would have hundreds of copies of my book Systematic Theology,[i] for example, but in a world with no money I would have no idea if one volume was worth a loaf of bread, or two shirts, or a bicycle, or a car. And the grocer might not be interested in reading my book, so he might not trade me a basket of groceries for even 100 books! Soon even the merchants who did accept my book in trade would not want another one, or a third one, and I would end up with piles of books and no ability to find more people who wanted to trade something for them. Without money, I would soon be forced to revert to subsistence living by planting a garden and raising cows and chickens, and maybe bartering a few eggs from time to time. And so would you, with whatever you could produce.

But money is the one thing that everybody is willing to trade goods for, because it is the one thing that everybody else is willing to trade goods for. With a system of money, I suddenly know how much one volume of my book is worth. It is worth $40, because that is how much thousands of people have decided they are willing to pay for it.

Money also stores the value of something until I spend it on something else. When I get the $40, that money temporarily holds the value of my book until I can go to the store and tell the grocer I would like to trade the $40 for some groceries. The same grocer who would not have traded any groceries for a theology book now eagerly accepts my $40 in money, because he knows that he can trade that money for anything in the world that he wants and that costs $40.

---

i   Wayne Grudem, *Systematic Theology: An Introduction to Biblical Doctrine* (Leicester: InterVarsity, 1994; Grand Rapids: Zondervan, 1994).

So money is simply a tool for our use, and we can rightly thank God that in his wisdom he ordained that we would invent it and use it. It is simply a "medium of exchange," something that makes voluntary exchanges possible. It is a commodity . . . that is legally established as an exchangeable equivalent of all other commodities, such as goods and services, and is used as a measure of their comparative values on the market.[ii]

Money makes voluntary exchanges more fair, less wasteful, and far more extensive. We need money in the world in order for us to be good stewards of the earth and to glorify God through using it wisely.

If money were evil in itself, then God would not have any. But he says, "The silver is mine, and the gold is mine, declares the LORD of hosts" (Hag. 2:8).

It all belongs to him, and he entrusts it to us so that through it we would glorify him.

Money provides many opportunities to glorify God: through investing and expanding our stewardship and thus imitating God's sovereignty and wisdom; through meeting our own needs and thus imitating God's independence; through giving to others and thus imitating God's mercy and love; or through giving to the church and to evangelism and thus bringing others into the kingdom.

Yet because money carries so much power and so much value, it is a heavy responsibility, and it presents constant temptations to sin. We can become ensnared in the love of money (1 Tim. 6:10), and it can turn our hearts from God. Jesus warned, "You cannot serve God and money"

---

ii   *The American Heritage Dictionary of the English Language* (Boston: Houghton Mifflin, 1992), 1166.

(Matt. 6:24), and he warned against accumulating too much that we hoard and do not use for good:

> *Do not lay up for yourselves treasures on earth, where moth and rust destroy and where thieves break in and steal, but lay up for yourselves treasures in heaven, where neither moth nor rust destroys and where thieves do not break in and steal. For where your treasure is, there your heart will be also. (Matt. 6:19-21)*

But the distortions of something good must not cause us to think that the thing itself is evil. Money is good in itself, and provides us many opportunities for glorifying God.

Prosperity Teachers

Our task in this book has been to address the core principles and ideas of prosperity teaching, rather than argue with particular preachers. But there are many influential people we have in mind who, in different ways and forms, have articulated and spread this prosperity gospel.

We could reference, for example, Duncan Williams, Benson Idahosa, David Oyedepo (founder of Winners Chapel), John Praise, Kenneth & Gloria Copeland, Kenneth Hagin, Marilyn Hickey, Morris Cerullo, John Avanzini, Robert Tilton, Benny Hinn, Charles Capps, Joel Osteen, and T.D. Jakes.

However, more than anything else, we encourage readers to examine the preaching they hear in the light of the Bible. We hope that this book has helped you to do that.

Further Reading: Other Books on Prosperity Teaching

Not enough has been written on this subject when you consider the impact it is having on churches around the world. We would like to challenge pastors and theologians to tackle this false teaching in writing.

Here are a few valuable books for further reading:

Adeleye, Femi *Preachers of a Different* Gospel (Hippo Books, 2011).

This Nigerian author seeks to examine the claims of the prosperity gospel, exposing the ways in which it contradicts the Bible. His book is a warning of the subtle ways in which this false teaching has infiltrated the church.

Fee, Gordon *The Disease of the Health and Wealth Gospels* (Vancouver: Regent College, 2006).

With his background as a New Testament scholar, Fee's exegesis enables him to specifically critique popular Christian approaches to the themes of health and wealth and prosperity. This helpful booklet points the reader to a biblically faithful position.

Hanegraaf, Hank *Christianity in Crisis: The 21st Century* (Nashville: Thomas Nelson, 2009).

Hanegraaf follows up on his influential 1993 book with a new effort to detail and expose the major errors of contemporary Christianity, while providing scriptural answers in each case.

Jones, David & Russell Woodbridge *Health, Wealth & Happiness* (Grand Rapids: Kregel 2011).

Jones & Woodbridge go back to the Scriptures to set forth a truly biblical understanding of wealth, poverty, suffering, and giving. They identify five crucial areas of error related to the prosperity gospel movement. This book challenges readers to rediscover the true gospel of Jesus.

McConnell, Dan *A Different Gospel: Updated Edition* (Peabody: Hendrickson, 1995).

With a pastor's heart and a scholar's eye, McConnell delves into the foundation of "name it and claim it" theology. In doing so, he demonstrates the dangers of its unbiblical teaching.

Associated Titles

Ferdinando, Keith *The Battle is God's* **(ACTS, 2012).**
Addressing spiritual warfare in an African context, this book deals with the issue of pain and suffering.

Rees, Stephen *Jesus: Suffering Saviour, Sovereign Lord* **(ACTS, 2012).**
This collection of papers focuses on the servant songs of Isaiah and Philippians chapter 2. These sermons, given at various conferences around the world, are full of Christ. They are excellent examples of how to handle the Word of God correctly, so that God's voice is truly heard. Such examples are greatly needed today, when so many twist the Bible to try and make it say whatever they want it to say.